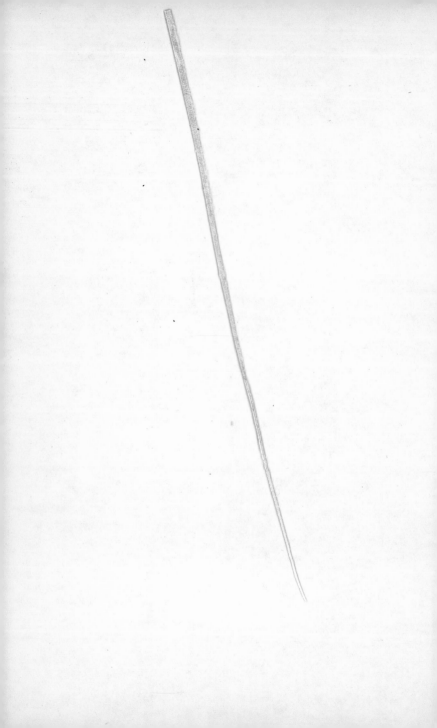

SUWANNEE RIVER
Strange Green Land

Books by

CECILE HULSE MATSCHAT

MEXICAN PLANTS
GARDEN CALENDAR

(GARDEN PRIMERS)
ANNUALS AND PERENNIALS
SHRUBS AND TREES
BULBS AND HOUSE PLANTS
PLANNING THE HOME GROUNDS
HOW TO MAKE A GARDEN

SUWANNEE RIVER: STRANGE GREEN LAND

SUWANNEE RIVER

Strange Green Land

by

Mrs. CECILE HULSE MATSCHAT

Illustrated by

ALEXANDER KEY

THE LITERARY GUILD OF AMERICA, INC.

New York, N. Y.

CL

TO

MOTHER AND DAD

Contents

CONTENTS

PART THREE. GULF FOLK

SUWANNEE RIVER

Strange Green Land

Way Down upon the SUWANNEE RIVER — Florida

The River

THE birthplace of the Suwannee is in Georgia, deep in the somber heart of the Okefenokee Swamp.

Grotesque, bottle-shaped cypress trees, sixty to ninety feet in height, with wide-spreading tops, reach upward from the wine-colored water and form a canopy so dense that only a weird green light dapples the floor of the forest. Everywhere long banners of Spanish moss hang down from the living trees, hiding their feathery foliage from the sight of man and covering up dead stumps. Through the vast drowned

3

swamp two tiny streams, faintly reflecting the eerie light, creep sluggishly to unite at last before a spit of quaking land.

The two streams, now one small current, move slowly between wild stretches of spongy earth. Often the low banks, which control the young river's course, retreat and its waters escape into the flooded wilderness, where trees struggle to exist and push knobby roots or "knees," four feet or so above the surface to help them breathe. Farther down, vines of arsenic green wall in the river, screening high mounds built by a long-dead race.

The Suwannee wanders slowly on its way, over the border of the great swamp and through a smaller one, named for the river. At Edith it picks up the Suwannoochee Creek, fringed with a sea of yellow-eyed grass, and then continues on its southwestern journey until it crosses the boundary line of Florida at Blounts Ferry. Wider now, the stream flows almost directly west between high banks lined with palms and live oaks, and on through the glade where Osceola, the famous Seminole chief, incited his followers to massacre the early settlers. Then it turns and twists through wide green valleys, justifying its Indian name of Winding River, and waters little farms and truck gardens. Near its junction with the Withlacoochee at Ellaville—marriage of Indian poetry to commercial Babbittry—the Alapaha pours into the brown tide now going more swiftly toward the sea. Flowing south, through towns which once bustled with activity, when great mills turned fragrant pine and cypress into two-by-fours and shingles, it presently adds the

Santa Fe to the volume of its waters. As the river widens and shallows in the lowlands, it slides past sleepy little hamlets of colored folk, who claim to be the descendants of runaway slaves led by a regal Ethiopian named King Nero. But soon it forsakes even these small human habitations to enter country reminiscent of its source springs, flooded hammocks and dense jungles. So, through two hundred and forty miles of varied land and climate, where spring comes before autumn ends, the Suwannee runs. Twelve miles north of Cedar Keys the Winding River empties into the Gulf of Mexico.

What is the origin of the word Suwannee? The Seminoles say that in early times they were ruled by a noble chieftainess, Su-wan-nee, whose name their ancestors gave to the river, so that the beloved woman might be remembered forever and her spirit live on with them. Never one legend but another rises to contradict it! It is also said that the Spanish called the river the Little St. John, and that Suwannee is merely a corruption of San Juanito.

Of all the rivers in America the Suwannee is the most romantic. It has a place beside the royal rivers of the world, though no New York, Paris, or London sprawls along its banks, and no torrential cataract appears in its course to challenge Niagara. In countries where the name of no other American stream is familiar, Stephen Foster's "Way Down upon the Suwannee River" is sung and loved.

But there is more to the Suwannee than a song. It has a story that is unique among American chronicles. It is said that the Mayas of Yucatán ascended

it and named it Water Beloved of the Sun God
long before Europeans visited our Southland. In the
shadow of the forests along its banks, Spanish priests
built missions and preached the gospel of the Cross.
Some of the fiercest battles of the Indian wars were
fought near its headwaters. Later, great cotton plantations and colonial mansions flourished in the river
valleys; and still later, after the Civil War, this gracious and abundant life of the lower river sank into
decay. These are all important episodes in the history
of the Suwannee. But the real story of the river,
new, and stranger than legend, is the story of the
almost unknown folk who inhabit the vast swampland in which the Suwannee rises.

The great majority of the earlier settlers in the
swamp region were English. Doubtless most of them
came from General Oglethorpe's settlement at Savannah and from Ebenezer, Darien, and Frederica; but
there were also men from other colonies, chiefly the
Carolinas, who preferred to hunt, fish, and trap
rather than to farm. The rest were French Huguenots,
Spanish from St. Augustine, Scotch-Irish, Salzburgers,
Moravians, and one pseudo Quaker, who won ever-
lasting infamy. He was Edmund Grey, an outlaw
from Virginia. As leader of a large band of debtors
and criminals, he founded the settlement of New
Hanover on the Satilla, a few miles from Okefenokee;
then, still in his guise of a gentle Quaker, he established another lawless colony on Cumberland Island.

The inhabitants of Okefenokee are among the
purest Anglo-Saxon stock in America. Their speech
retains the flavor of the language of Elizabethan times,

which was still spoken commonly in England when General Oglethorpe brought his first colony to Georgia. The secluded life has kept intact their legacy from the mother country of the sixteenth century. But the mild climate and the profusion of fish and game and the two-season crops so easily raised in the swampland have produced, from the old stock, a distinct race of folk.

The English-speaking settlers of the river basin migrated from Alabama, Georgia, South Carolina, the mid-Atlantic colonies, and even from far-off Maine. They went to the South to take advantage of its fertile lands and mild climate: in the valleys grew some of the finest sea-island cotton and sugar in the world. They brought with them indentured servants, who served from two to six years, and Negro slaves.

Yet, in spite of their diverse origin, all these people have much in common. They are cantankerous and cussed and quick to anger. And they are wise and witty, with a store of odd superstitions and shrewd sayings.

But the swamp folk are the wilder breed, wary as the four-footed, light-treading felines of their region, and deeply suspicious of the rare visitor from the "outland," not solely because they instinctively believe him to be a "revenooer." They are a law unto themselves, and their elemental code has its own primitive machinery. They want little to do with the complex statutes of the outland, sometimes also called Ameriky, which makes no sense to them; and they have small welcome for "city fowkses," whom they suspect of looking down on them or seeking to poach on their rights.

Physically, they are strong and sturdy, with splendid health and high spirits; a tall, handsome people, slim, rangy, and hard. Close intermarriage during two centuries and more has not weakened the stock. Okefenokee breeds no morons. Though book larnin' is hardly known among swamp people, they have intelligent minds, sharp and shrewd. They are totally unlike the crackers of *Tobacco Road*, or any of the traditional poor whites. The swamp is free of hookworm, pellagra, and malaria. The malarial mosquito does not breed in Okefenokee, and other species, where they exist at all, are very scarce. Perhaps the swamp water is made too acid by the cypresses; perhaps its constant movement—stirred, the swampers say, by myriad springs—prevents the growth of mosquito larvae. There is no slimy, stagnant water; and certainly there is a current—take in pole, or paddle, anywhere and the boat drifts, so they say, always toward the Suwannee.

For their security in a jungle infested with menace, the swamp folk have learned to be keen observers of all wild life, plant life as well. Their women love flowers and gather herbs for seasonings and medicines. So a woman interested in botany and the study of birds and reptiles could come among them without arousing their suspicion and hostility, even though she was from the outland. The Plant Woman, as they called her, fitted naturally into their lives.

PART ONE
Swamp Folk

The
Birthplace
of the
Suwannee
OKEFENOKEE
WILDLIFE
REFUGE
GEORGIA

OKEFENOKEE

SAPLING PRAIRIE

DINNER POND

MINNIE ISLANDS

BIG WATER L.

FLOYD IS. PRAIRIE

FLOYD ISLAND

ROWELLS IS.

BILLYS L.

CHASE PRAIRIE

PINE IS.

SUWANNEE R.

THE POCKET

NEW IS.

BILLYS IS.

ROADS

SUWANNEE CANAL

CAMP CORNELIA

HONEY IS.

BUGABOO IS.

SWAMP

STRANGE IS.

GRAND PRAIRIE

FIDDLERS IS.

BOAT RUN

SUWANNEE RIVER

BLACK JACK IS.

MITCHELLS IS.

BROOMSTRAW IS.

SOLDIERS CAMP

GEORGIA
FLORIDA

1 5
MILES

ST. MARYS RIVER

TRAIL RIDGE

CHAPTER ONE

Okefenokee

ALL through the night weird voices shriek and howl in the darkness. But in the pale hour before dawn, when the radiance of the stars is dimmed, not even the flutter of a leaf breaks the silence. The fierce night hunters, the felines and deadly snakes, have retreated to their lairs; the deer, the myriad birds, and other wild creatures of the day are not yet astir. For mornglowm is the hour when hants roam the swamp country; and few things living dare to venture forth.

In the east a barrier of misty rose piles up and a few cloudlets become tinged with yellow, in the center of a pale green sky. Suddenly, a rim of flaming gold gleams above the horizon and the east is tinted orange, then red, then crimson. Another day has begun. With the coming of sunlight the silence is broken and there is noise and movement everywhere.

It is spring in the Okefenokee wilderness—the time of late-blooming Cherokee roses and yellow jessamine—and for that reason the chorus of wild life in the great swamp swells louder than usual. White egrets, nesting in the bays at the edge of the marsh, make the air ring with their chuckling calls and the beating of their wings. Giant cranes flap up from the wide water prairies and rain down volleys of loud, whooping trumpet notes upon a lone blue heron, standing on one leg in the shallows. The deep, coughing grunt of a black bear hunting breakfast sounds from the fastness of an islet. Presently a huge bull gator thunders forth a challenge to others of his kind; and alligator after alligator answers, until the swamp for miles about resounds with the hideous clamor of their bellowing.

But one such spring morning two persons in a small, flat-bottomed skiff in the heart of the swamp did not hear the music of the wild, nor see the beauty of the gloomy water and the occasional ray of light that silvered the gray-tressed cypress and shimmered on the green bay leaves. Their attention was fixed on a big cottonmouth basking on a cypress root—knee, the swampers call it—which protruded above the water about the height of the Plant Woman's head. The bow of the boat, where she sat, had brushed against the knee and stopped, fortunately without shaking it. She held herself rigid and gazed steadily into the reptile's black, unwinking eyes. Freeman, the swamper, stood in the stern. With his three-pronged pole thrust into the miry bed of the shallow run, he edged the boat backward, inch by inch. She knew that her life depended on his skill. One slip of the pole and the boat would jar heavily against the knee; then the hideous chunky head would slash forward and strike its fangs, an inch long and needlesharp, into her face. But gently, and so slowly that it seemed to her motionless on the leaf-brown water, the boat slid away and the deadly snake lay quiet.

In the center of the run Freeman sat down and wiped his face. "Lotsa varmints out this spring." He spat into the water. "Purty, hain't he!"

"No," said the shuddering Plant Woman. "It has horrid eyes!" She was out of danger from the fangs now, but the close view of the eyes had produced its own chill of horror: like many venomous snakes, the cottonmouth has eyes of a shoe-button black, with no perceptible iris, the elliptical pupil like a thin vertical line of a cold jade green. This line expands in darkness and gives the eyes their brilliance during nocturnal hunting. "Shoot it!" she demanded, indignant because Freeman sat so calmly, chewing his tobacco.

"What for?" He shoved off down the run. "Thar's thousands of 'em in the swamp. Hain't no use to git rid of jest one. An' sides, thar's plenty things wars on 'em, as is meant to do."

That was the Plant Woman's introduction to Okefenokee, the almost unknown wilderness which is nearly as wild and untamed today as it was thousands of years ago. It is a great gray world of flooded land and water, inhabited by innumerable birds, by huge bears and wild swine, alligators and snakes, and primitive human beings who pole their boats under the cypresses and prowl like wild men. It was also her first opportunity to know Freeman, who was to be her guide in Okefenokee. His wife was one who knew herbs and simples, and she had opened their cabin home to the Plant Woman.

Freeman was a tall man with square shoulders and a square jaw covered with a thick, bushy growth of jet-black hair. "Grow-an'-be-damned," he'd say, staring into his bit of mirror, "blest if ye-all don' make me a fierce looker, all hairy like," and he would comb his whiskers admiringly until they stood out in a thick mass from his brown face, and curl up the ends of his sweeping mustache. His shrewd countenance was unlined by his fifty years and his twinkling blue eyes were young with the unworried look of one who had found it easy to live off the land. Instinctively, at sight, strangers respected Freeman. Among the swamp folk he was a leader. There was something vital and earthy about him that appealed to them, and he wronged no one.

The boat glided on. Hours of travel lay ahead before nightfall and the exciting event of the Plant Woman's first visit to a still in the haunts of the wilderness moonshiners. All day they poled and paddled through the great swamp, over the still water prairies and along the runs—slow currents winding around islands and through the deeper cypress bays—then down a twisting waterway and across a wide marsh, where tidal creeks flowed to the sea. Dusk fell and deepened over the low country, but Freeman pushed steadily on. The woman knew she could never find her way out, alone. Suddenly, he turned and said, in an apologetic tone, "Course, I spoke for ye, but een so, my friend wants ye should kiver yer eyes, jest while we go inside. Says I, 'Course she won't kyar! She's got lotsa sense, even if she be from the outland. An' ye know she ain't no revenooer. She be a-huntin' weeds an' flowers an' sich in the big swamp, een supposin' thar beint no sense to it.' "

He stopped paddling and took something from his pocket. The woman, startled, drew back. " 'T won't hurt ye noan, ma'am. Hain't no call to be skeert. Ole Pappy, he don' trust outlanders noan, that's all." He tied a crude bandage across her eyes. Then he shoved on, while his passenger sat motionless and almost breathless in her enforced blindness, with only the senses of feeling and hearing left free and her imagination—stimulated hours before by the cottonmouth—inclined to overwork. She heard the brushing of reeds against the sides of the skiff. Frogs croaked and strange birds called, and she felt sea mists roll in from the Atlantic.

At last there were voices. Freeman helped her from the boat, but other hands felt over her for weapons. "Step along, Plant Woman, don' be skeert."

She stumbled along a little path; men on both sides held her arms and prevented her from falling over roots and logs. "Stand still," and she heard the roar and crackle of a blazing fire. The bandage was removed and the light showed a row of men's faces turned upon her intently. There were no women. Freeman had disappeared.

A tall, bright-faced boy with sharp eyes stepped forward by the side of a big man who carried a rifle slung loosely in the crook of his arm. "This is Pappy, ma'am," the boy said and walked away. Slowly the Plant Woman's eyes traveled over the large frame, the thick, gray-white hair and heavy, close-set growth of beard, and met hard gray eyes, looking out fiercely, searchingly, from beneath bushy brows.

"Howdy, Plant Woman." He spat into the fire. "Heerd tell as how ye want to see a still. Not that I is sayin' as thar is one, an' not that I is sayin' as thar hain't. Let's set, an' git a-known. Whar be ye from?"

"New York." The woman sat upon an empty box. "Have you ever been there?"

"Nuvver heerd of hit. Don' take ary truck with the outland."

There was silence for a while. The little man, Dave, moved uneasily. "Is that town big as," he hesitated a moment, "big as Moniac?"

They were really interested, the Plant Woman thought complacently. "Oh, yes! New York must be at least ten thousand times as large."

"Ten thousand!" Dave breathed hard through his nose.

Big Bill spat at a log, missed, and tried again

with better aim. "How many fowkses in New Yawk?"

The Plant Woman was not certain. "Probably four or five millions," she ventured boldly.

Pappy growled deeply. "Fowkses must live in bunches! How be it they git aroun'?"

"Well, a great many people ride under the ground in trains that run through tunnels—subways, we call them—while others ride in cars above the ground. Then there are bridges over all the rivers, so that the people can pass easily from one part of the city to another, and tunnels beneath some of the rivers for motorcars to use."

Isaac's scarred face twisted in a knowing grin. "By heck, that's a hot one! How many motykyars go through 'em?"

The woman was getting into deep water. "I don't know, exactly. Millions, I suppose, eventually."

Pappy sniffed disapprovingly. "Whar all these fowkses live, as has so many motykyars?"

"Some live in the suburbs, small towns like Moniac, a few miles away from New York. But most of the people live in tall buildings, which are divided into separate apartments or homes, one on top of the other—like this!" With a twig she drew a cross section of an apartment house in the fire-lighted sand.

All the heads craned forward to look. "Like a bee gum," Dave ventured.

"Bee gum? Oh, a beehive. Yes, something like that."

" 'Spect the fowkses git right smart tired havin' to crawl flat like," Pappy said, slyly.

"Oh, no! Look! The buildings are very tall, and the rooms of each home are as tall as those of your cabins, so the people walk upright, exactly as you do. They don't crawl. Why, the place I live in is more than a hundred and fifty feet high!"

They all stared, disbelief written plainly on their faces. Big Bill took a deep breath. "Yon tree—" he pointed a dirty hand dramatically at a cypress, "yon tree is moren eighty foot." He glared menacingly at the Plant Woman. She nodded. "Well, whar ye live is tall as two treeses, jined togither? Hain't nuvver!"

Silence for a while. Dave cleared his throat. "Tell some more, Plant Woman," he begged politely.

The harassed woman glanced around. Shrewd eyes in grinning faces stared intently at her, waiting.

"There is a beautiful garden on the roof of the house where I live. It took tons of earth to make the foundation for the garden, to get enough soil for the things to grow in."

Again there was silence. "What grows thar, ma'am, so high up like?" Dave wanted to know. He was still the quintessence of politeness.

The Plant Woman was on firm ground now. "Oh, almost anything," she explained happily, "corn, cabbage, cauliflower, all kinds of flowers—and trees."

Big Bill stood up and snapped his suspenders loudly. "Treeses!" he said, spat in disgust, and walked away.

Pappy rose without a word, lighted a pine torch at the fire, and strode down a little path, beckoning the woman to follow. A faint, sickish odor came over the tops of the bay trees, and the sound of voices and laughter. He dropped on all fours and crawled through a low, tunnellike opening in the thicket. The Plant Woman crept after him into the clearing.

The light from flaring torches showed a dozen men grouped around a big cooker of copper and hardwood which stood above a stone fireplace. Other men were taking turns at catching drinks in gourds. A pipe protruded from the cover of the pot and connected the cooker with the worm, or coils, immersed in a barrel of cold water. The copper pot glowed with a fierce heat, and the men fed the fire with small hickory chips. Scattered here and there lay empty meal sacks. To one side were a few barrels of mash, boiling and bubbling in various stages of fermentation; on some the heads had formed, covering the surface with foam and tiny floating particles. One barrel was nearly full of a clear, sour-smelling liquid. "Beer," said one of the men, answering the Plant Woman's question, "nigh unto thirty per cent."

"Alcohol?" she asked in surprise.

"Sure 'nough." He pushed back the brim of his hat and dipped out a tin cup full. At her refusal, he drank deeply. "Catawumpus! Kin lick my weight in wildcats, after that."

Pappy picked up a gourd and held it under the trickle of warm white liquid that dripped from a pipe near the bottom of the barrel. He drank half a cup of the green corn liquor as though it were water, then gallantly wiped the rim on his sleeve, refilled it, and handed it to the Plant Woman. Not to be outdone, and in fear of offending him, she took a good swallow—then choked and gasped for breath, while tears ran down her cheeks. The undiluted liquid, strong as pure alcohol, was like a draught of fire. "Swell," she managed, handing the gourd back to him. "Thank you very much for showing me your still."

"Shucks, 't ain't nothin', Plant Woman. I hain't nuvver heerd tell of no lady revenooer. I'd like it real smart iffen ye'd kyar to bide awhile. Wouldn't be ary diffikilty, an' ye got no call to be skeert. Nary one 'ud dast lay a finger on ye."

"I'd like very much to stay sometime, if your wife could make room for me. I'm not familiar with this part of the country at all. But the boys didn't approve of me. I don't think they believed me."

"Hain't nary need to worrit about 'em, ma'am. Course, it might be best iffen ye warn't sich a gol-busted yarner. But thar, Plant Woman, don' ye be a-carin'. 'T ain't yer fault," he added, kindly. "Ye're a womern."

Then he blindfolded her and led her back to the boat. "Black as pitch now, reckon ye'd best take it off," Freeman said and glided out into the run. A couple of hours of poling brought them to an island where several families lived. They spent the night there. Next morning the Plant Woman began her exploration of the big swamp.

The swamp covers about seven hundred square miles of territory and is even today almost as much of a mystery as the Forbidden Country of the Amazon. Many persons are born, live, and die almost within sight of Okefenokee, yet never dare to venture across its borders. Fantastic legends are told of its horrors, and facts even more fantastic than the legends have never been told. One tale has it that on stormy nights the ghost of a slave ship—*La Estrellita*—sails up the St. Marys River, a prong of which extends into the swamp. She is manned by the skeletons of long-dead seamen, who abandon their contraband cargo on the hidden islands. The clanking of slave chains can be heard clearly on still nights! The visitor may hear, too, of phantom deer and panthers roaming the piney woods in the moonlight. They can be killed only by bullets made of cow, or horse, hair: ordinary bullets are dangerous, because they rebound from the thick hides of the animals and kill the hunters so foolhardy as to use them. But even were these fantasies true, they would be less mysterious than the vast trembling ground which is Okefenokee in fact.

Among southern fresh-water swamps only the Everglades in Florida is larger than Okefenokee. It is roughly forty-five miles in length by thirty in width, irregular in shape, and covers parts of six counties, four in Georgia and two in Florida. The Seminole Indians, who once lived in the swamp, called it "ecunnau finocau"—earth trembling. Old maps show many variations of this spelling, down to the present-day form. The swamp folk and geographical authorities pronounce the word "Oke-e-fen-oke," leaving the final *ee* silent.

Different theories have been advanced to account for the origin of the swamp. One theory is that some upheaval of the earth caused a ridge to be thrown up across the Suwannee Strait—which, ages ago, sup-

posedly separated Florida from the mainland—and
thus formed a shallow inland sea. Through the centuries this sea gradually filled with vegetation. The
swamp dwellers claim that the marsh is full of springs,
for even during times of severe drought the water
never falls below a certain level.

Entrance to the swamp is impossible except
through the regular channels, and sometimes these
are difficult of access, as they become choked with
rotted logs and other debris. To reach the heart of
the swamp from Cowhouse Island, on the north edge,
requires an entire day's steady poling through the
dark runs and over the flower-decked prairies. Another entrance is by way of Folkston and the Suwannee Canal, commonly known as Jackson's Folly,
which extends from the St. Marys River about twelve
miles into the swamp. The interior can be reached
also from Fargo, by way of Mixon's Ferry on the
Suwannee, the Pocket, across Jones Island, and over
a thousand-foot path of single rotted planks, nine
inches wide, nailed to fallen trees and decaying stumps
a few feet above the water of the marsh.

To save hours of hard poling on a broiling hot
day, with the temperature in the swamp at more than
a hundred degrees, Freeman and the Plant Woman
crossed this boardwalk to reach Billys Lake. Freeman,
with the free, effortless movements of the swamp
folk, trotted ahead across the rickety planks as casu-
ally as though no alligators, alligator snappers, and
cottonmouths inhabited the waters of the marsh. The
woman followed slowly, one booted foot set down
with care directly ahead of the other. A quarter of
the way across she stopped to rest beside a tall, slim

bush which grew close to the board path. Holding to a trailing branch, she looked across the swamp. The sun burned her back through her thin cotton shirt and turned the brown water to molten copper, where flat pads of water lilies floated and the golden club lifted its tall spears. In the shallows, near the bays, a fragrant pink orchid with a bearded lip had opened thousands of delicate blossoms, and under the shadows of the trees masses of wild callas held up their pure white trumpets. Red-winged blackbirds tilted on every tussock and filled the air with their shrill, tuneless music. It all looked safe and peaceful. Reassured, she started on, answering Freeman's impatient hail with a cheerful response.

Halfway across, the planks were rotted and broken, and the bridge swayed with every step. Here and there great patches of hammock soil lifted above the low water and the rank green growth was so tall and lush that the narrow path appeared to curve on and on through a waving sea of grass. The Plant Woman hesitated, looked down, and was lost. A brilliant banded water snake swam with graceful, curving movements across a little pool. It disappeared into the grass, which waved sinuously *against* the play of the wind, as Freeman had told her it would. This sign of "the snake in the grass" is carefully noted by swampers; it is important to their safety.

Afraid to go forward and unable to go back, the woman stood, balanced precariously, arms outthrust like a tightrope walker, a camera clutched in one hand and a notebook in the other. The board beneath her feet creaked protestingly at her weight and seemed to sag closer to the water. The notebook dropped from her fingers and fell upon a patch of oozy muck and golden-yellow water weeds. Instantly a whole section of the marsh heaved upward and an evil, reptilian head, large as a small football, with glittering eyes and snapping beak, lunged viciously at her booted foot. With a yell she sprang forward and raced down the boardwalk.

Swamp folk are as much afraid of the ferocious alligator snappers as they are of the real alligators. Quick as a snake in striking, a gator snapper can amputate a man's hand with one bite of its steellike jaws. Large snappers may weigh a hundred pounds, and it is claimed that they live for more than a century. The shell is the color of the brown muck where they lie in wait for their food. Many an unsuspecting waterfowl is caught and dragged down to furnish a meal for the gator snapper.

Okefenokee provides no ground for permanent human habitation except on a few of the larger islands: Billys, Floyd, Cowhouse, Black Jack, Mitchells, Honey, and Bugaboo. Men have lived on all of these at some time or other, and one hears also of lost islands. There are only a few islands in the swamp where people live at present; the rest of the folk are scattered along its borders. They are areas of sandy soil above the average level of the water and range in size from one to ten square miles. The rest of the swamp is perpetually flooded. Even in times of severe drought only a small portion of it is penetrable on foot; the quivering earth is so insecure that the tread of a man will cause an eighty-foot cypress to tremble like an aspen. Most of the swamp ground is nothing more than a mass of twisted roots covered with a little sand and a few feet of leaf mold.

Some of the magnificent longleaf pine of the larger islands has been cut by lumber companies, but so much still remains that Okefenokee is almost as primitive as though no ax had touched it. It is surrounded by the typical flat, piney woods of the Deep South, but the hammocks on the islands are very different in character from the piney woods of the outland. In the hammocks the live oaks and the sweet gums drop their cast-off leaves year after year upon the virgin soil which lies several feet deep in leaf mold. In the spring, for countless generations, the green blossoms of the red bay and the creamy petals of the magnolia have drifted down like shadows upon the cool earth. Here water oaks and hardwood and pines and hollies all reach their ultimate size, living out their life span to sink down at last in dignity and solitude; while saplings sprout from the rich mold around their roots, to carry on the race. The saw palmetto, a small fan palm, creeps beneath the trees, with gorgeous long blooms of ivory white; later in the year it bears luscious black fruit which was a favorite food of the Indians'.

Wild muscadines grow lustily in the cool damp ness. The swamp folk come eagerly to gather these sweet, thick-skinned "grapes" from which they make their famous scuppernong wine—heady and aromatic, like no other wine in the world. Pale blueberries flourish in the acid soil and blackberries twine in thorny masses on the edges of the hammocks, where the summer sun shines down.

Hammock growth usually covers the smaller islands and borders most of the larger ones. "Good-God" woodpeckers, with black and white wings and scarlet crests, and two other woodpeckers, called "white-shirts" and "cham-chacks," work with a continuous *r-r-r-rat-a-tat-tat-tat*. These are local names given them by the swampers to describe the individual sounds the birds make either in tapping their favorite trees, or calling in flight. Cham-chack and white-shirt peck cypress. Good-God is a hardwood tapper. Carolina wrens are common, cardinals or red birds move about with dignity, usually in pairs, and the yellow-tailed bee bird and the tickbird, both flycatchers, sing from some shady retreat on the hottest day in summer.

In the pine barrens of the islands the wild turkey, the wariest fowl in the swamp, makes its home in company with mourning doves, nighthawks, an occasional chuck-will's-widow, and dozens of other birds.

Cypress ponds a few feet deep are found in most of the pine barrens. There typical swamp trees grow vigorously: cypress, slash pine, black gum, sweet bay, and yaupon, a beautiful evergreen holly with vivid scarlet berries. These ponds are often the home of one or more gators and of small fish, such as killifish, and various species of frogs. During droughts they dry up and the gators and frogs escape to the deep water of the bays; but the fish are caught with no way of reaching water, and die and rot beneath the burning sun. Then the stifling smell of rotting fish and decaying vegetation rises from the burned grasses and dried mud of the islands, and there the night-hunting venomous snakes congregate in the dark by scores.

In the evening, or after a warm rain, the frog orchestra turns out in full force. Each species has its own peculiar song and pitch; and much of the really primitive folk music of Okefenokee is borrowed from its frogs and toads. The swampers call the frog music the Song of Okefenokee and imitate it in their signal calls, and in the songs without words that they sing in long hours of poling down the runs.

More than two dozen species of snakes are known to live in the hammocks and piney woods of the islands. Six are deadly poisonous; three kinds of rattlesnakes—the diamondback, the timber or Seminole (which the swamp folk insist is the "wife of the diamondback"), and the small ground rattler; the cottonmouth or water moccasin, much more numerous than all the rattlesnakes and even more dangerous for it gives no warning of its presence; the copperhead, rare in this region; and the lovely coral snake, which belongs to the cobra family and injects its venom by biting instead of striking. Some of the folk make a business of collecting rattlesnake skins for sale in the outland, where snake shoes and accessories are the fashion for ladies. The swampers cook the flesh for the oil, which they prize highly as a remedy for rheumatism.

Other snake species in Okefenokee are non-poisonous. The Plant Woman, however, could never make up her mind whether it was worse to perish from snake bite or to be scared to death. Once, innocently absorbed in gathering water lilies, she found herself the unexpected possessor of a bracelet of velvety brown snake with brilliant sulphur-yellow stripes and golden-red eyes. This was only one of the tiny ribbon snakes that live among the lily blossoms.

A harmless spreading adder, locally called the "possum," puts on such a ferocious appearance when disturbed that the swampers firmly believe it to be poisonous. But call possum's bluff, and it flops over and plays dead! Withdraw a few steps, and it turns on its belly and hastens to crawl out of sight; make a startling move, and it plays dead again. Among other interesting and harmless snakes are the king snake, which wars on rattlesnakes and other reptiles; the beautiful bluish indigo snake, often eight feet long in Okefenokee; and the black snake. Nonpoisonous serpents hunt by day. Their eyes differ in appearance from those of the venomous species: they are round and full, that is, they protrude more, and usually have a dark brown iris and black pupil.

The swampers have an amusing superstition about the black snake.

"Plant Woman," said Freeman, "I'd take hit right kindly iffen ye'd hearken to the black snake a-hollerin' in the bog lot. Why, I've heerd tell as how Gre'-gre'-gran'paw—as how everybody 'lows was a plump smart feller from fureen shores—was a-tolled way into the swamp an' came mighty nigh unto death's door by a-listenin' to jest sich. Ye be warned, ma'am, an' shet yer ears quick, iffen so be ye hear one a-singin'!"

"What do you mean, Freeman? I don't hear anything but the frogs."

"Frogs nothin', beggin' yer pardon, ma'am. That thar's a black snake a-hollerin'. Why, jest t-other day I heerd one, an' went as clost as I dast, an' thar he be, a-singin' a lullaby so sweet it seemed like I jest had to foller him. But I knew 't was a trick, ma'am, an' resisted his wiles. Ole diamondback is his pal. They live togither in winter an' the black one a-tolls people in to whar the rattler can nip 'em, ma'am."

"Why should the black snake do that?" asked

the Plant Woman. "Surely not just to have a home in winter, with so many empty logs around."

Freeman studied on this for a while. "Well," he said finally, "I reckon hit's this a-way. Thar's a passel o' things here all swarved up togither. Some 'pear set on raisin' a crop o' trouble, an' rookus like pizen, but others is peaceable as mournin' doves, a-nestin' like ole diamondback an' the black. See that bee?" A stubby finger pointed at a bumblebee zooming above a stalk of palmetto blossoms. "Know why bumblebees alus makes more long sweetnin' than tame bees? I'll tell ye. Hit's 'cause they has the co-operativeness of lightnin' bugs. That's why! The Injuns, they was smart boogers; an' bein' extry fond of long sweetnin', they got a couple of bumblebees an' wedded 'em to lightnin' bugs, so they could work in the dark. Now, hain't that somethin'?"

In the weird, hobgoblin world of the bays there is perpetual twilight. These bays are flooded forests of close-growing cypresses mixed with a few other trees. They stretch away from the prairies and runs into unexplored depths of shadow and mystery. Even at midday, with a brilliant sun overhead, only an occasional ray pierces the thick green roof of the jungle, spotting the brown water with flecks of gold and lightening the blue of the iris that blooms in the marginal shallows. The bottle-shaped trunks of the cypresses, often twelve feet in diameter at the base and a scant two feet in diameter above the swelling, where they begin to tower symmetrically toward the sky, gleam in tints of olive, silver, violet, and odd greens and blues. Their dark roots protrude above the surface of the water, either arched like bows or in groups of knees. Seeing this malformed forest in the strange green light, one might expect it to be the home of gnomes, with beards and humps. As a matter of fact, it is inhabited by much more sinister personalities.

The bays are the favorite haunts of the cottonmouths and other water snakes, which lie coiled contentedly on the cypress knees, or crawl into the bushes along the runs to sun themselves. Often they drop into the boats of the swamp folk as they pole beneath them. While the terrified boatman looks on in horror, the snake raises its menacing head, hisses angrily, and then—if this is the boatman's lucky day—glides slowly over the side into the water. Full-grown cottonmouths are four or five, and rarely six, feet long, a dull olive brown in color and not more than nine inches in circumference. Sometimes great masses of snakes, the harmless, brightly colored ones looped with the poisonous moccasins, are twined around dead limbs overhanging the runs. The Plant Woman saw hundreds of them hanging from the undersides of small bridges, also, as she journeyed down the Suwannee.

Deer, bears, wildcats, foxes, otters, raccoons, possums, and other animals abound in the swamp region. Panthers are still reported. A Florida wolf was killed as late as 1910, and the howl of another was heard in 1916. No one knows what wild life may be hidden deep in the swamp. Recently the round-tailed muskrat, or Florida water rat, has been found in Okefe-

nokee, the only place it is known to exist in Georgia.
The ivory-billed woodpecker, nearly extinct, lived
recently on Minnie Islands, and is doubtless still somewhere in the wild interior; the pileated woodpecker is
common. Sandhill cranes, limpkins, and other rare
birds make their home on the islands and prairies.

Egrets breed in the swamp country by the hundreds.
Wood ducks are seen the year round; and large flocks
of migratory birds, such as the hooded merganser,
mallard, black duck, green-winged teal, pintail, ring-
necked duck, woodcock, and Wilson's snipe, visit the
swamp during the winter months.

Through the winding runs in the bays the hunters follow the large black Florida bear, which often
weighs five hundred pounds. The thorny thickets
along the shores of the bays do not bother his tough
hide, but they keep out the deer, which frequent
only the open prairies and wooded islands. Marsh rab-

bits, that swim like ducks and have heavier fur than other species, are thick along the runs and in the sphagnum bogs.

Millions of sundews and pitcher plants bloom in the bogs and prairies. The small pitcher plant lifts its spotted leaves at least three feet into the air, while its blossoms look like tiny golden parasols below them. Here, too, the swamp folk come to gather the foliage of the leather or lather bush, which makes an excellent substitute for soap when crushed and worked to a lather in water. Ferns grow rank in all the marshy spots. Bamboo-brier or smilax vines drape their green over low and tall trees alike.

Hidden deep in the heart of the great swamp are small lakes. Some of them, like Billys Lake and the Big Water, are several miles long but very narrow; they are really only broader and deeper passages in the runs near the source of the Suwannee River. This is the most beautiful part of Okefenokee, with the little lakes gleaming like emeralds in their setting of close-ranked cypresses draped in moss. Hardwood, in late spring, is a mass of tiny white blossoms. Around the swollen bases of the trees grow high-bush huckleberries, their luscious fruit drooping over the wine-colored water to reflect in its surface. The swampers go a-berryin' by boat, keeping a wary eye out for cottonmouths and other snakes in the bushes.

Around the lake borders are thousands of golden bonnets and purple bladderwort. Dozens of alligators sun themselves on half-submerged logs among the flowers. Hundreds of others inhabit the runs and cypress bays, and the ponds on the islands. Some of the best fresh-water fishing in the Deep South is on the Suwannee and in the swamp. A recorded catch for one season from Suwannee Lake, near the river's headwaters, totaled 41,618 fish, of which two hundred were caught in one hour. In the swamp alone over thirty species of fish are found. The rain-fish, supposed to be one of the rarest in the world, breeds there in millions.

The prairies—the swamp folk's name for the open flooded marshes—are filled with a tropical luxuriance of water plants and resemble wide grassy meadows. They are dotted with wooded islets, commonly called "houses" because they have enough dry land to furnish camp sites for the hunters of deer, bear, wildcats, raccoon, otter, and other small animals that live in the swamp. Maiden cane grows in dense green masses three or four feet high, and there rice rats and Florida water rats, together with the bittern, make their nests. Katydids sway on the green tips in the sunshine and dive from them into the cool water. Gators travel over the prairies from one pool to another, through acres of white and gold water lilies, beds of cream-white arrowheads and bluish pickerelweed. They are often the swamper's trail blazers; the boatman finds easier poling down the lanes that the gators have opened through the thick reeds and water plants.

CHAPTER TWO

Mound Builders and Giants

"H<small>IT</small>'s jest like paradise when the roses is in bloom." Freeman broke a spray from a late-blooming bush where one solitary Cherokee rose gleamed among

the green leaves. The Plant Woman nodded, noticing
that thousands of the bushes lined the banks. Some
of them had climbed twelve or fifteen feet into the
trees, and dropped long festoons toward the ground.
Today Freeman had guided her to that sharp channel
which the St. Marys River sends into Okefenokee.

"I wish I knew how that rose came to Georgia,"
she mused, half to herself. "China is such a long way,
and it grows wild here as freely as in its native land."

Freeman coughed loudly. "Scuse me, ma'am.
Thar hain't no Chiny rose growin' here in Okefenokee.
Thar is a powerful generation of we-uns whose
fowkses came from a far an' ancient land called England, but none of we-uns came from Chiny."

"No, of course not. But the same rose grows
wild in China, too. How do you suppose it came to
be here in the swamp? Georgia has made it the state
flower."

"Can't help that, Plant Woman," he said stubbornly, "hit belongs to the swamp, all right. An' hit
was planted right here on the riverbanks by a Injun
gal. Ye like 'nough don't know much about such
things, bein' a fureen womern. Howsomever, hit ain't
fitten ye should be mis*in*formed. Ye see, a Injun boy
from this 'ere swamp was captured by some other
Injuns who had a upscuddle with 'em, an' they took
him outland and doomed him to die by fire in the
mornglowm. But he was took sick—'pears like he
couldn't stand nothin'—an' a Cherokee gal nussed
him right back to health. Well, they perked right
up to each other an' one day she told him how she
loved him an' they fled togither, come night. Afore

she left she picked a sprig of the white rose climbin' aroun' her pappy's door, an' brought hit with her and stuck hit in the ground. 'Spect, so she wouldn't be homesick. An' hit's bin here ever since. Ye see, hit ain't got nothin' to do with Chiny."

"No. I have been misinformed," the Plant Woman admitted.

There is another plant of the swamp country that has a more factual history but not, for the botanist, less romance. This is the Franklinia. Like the swamp people, Franklinia has little use for the outland. It is one of the rarest plants in the world, never found except in its native haunt near the Altamaha River, north of Okefenokee. It has lived like a hermit for more than a hundred and fifty years. Botanists and naturalists have searched for it in vain in the other swamps of southern Georgia; no specimen has ever been found there.

John Bartram, Royal Botanist to King George III of England, traveled with his son William through the Carolinas and Georgia into Florida, following the waterways and blazed Indian trails. On one of their trips they discovered this rare plant, which fascinated them with its pure white blooms and deep green leaves; the leaves turn brilliant crimson in the fall. They named it Franklinia, in honor of Benjamin Franklin.

William Bartram published the first known description of the big swamp. He did not venture into it, but skirted along its edge on the famous trail ridge from Savannah to Florida. Settlers, traders, and Indians told him tales of its horrors; and in his *Travels,* printed in 1791, he described it with a curious mixture of fact and fancy:

. . . a vast lake or marsh, called Ouaquaphenogaw . . . occupies a space of near three hundred miles in circuit . . . they [the Creeks] say it is inhabited by a peculiar race of Indians whose women are incomparably beautiful . . . this terrestrial paradise has been seen by . . . hunters when in pursuit of game, who being lost in inextricable swamps and bogs, and on the point of perishing, were unexpectedly relieved by . . . daughters of the sun, who . . . enjoined them to fly for safety . . . for that their husbands were fierce men, and cruel to strangers . . . these hunters had a view of their settlements, situated on the elevated banks of an island . . . in a beautiful lake; but . . . like inchanted land . . . it seemed to fly before them . . . [they] never having been able to find again that enchanting spot . . . yet they frequently met with certain signs of its being inhabited, as the building of canoes . . .

The enchanted city was a myth; the great swamp was a fact. Yet for more than fifty years after Bartram wrote his fascinating account, Okefenokee was left alone, the haunt of reptiles and of birds, and the sanctuary of men who were out of temper with their more conservative brethren in the settlements.

Freeman sat quietly, half asleep, letting the boat drift with the current. The Plant Woman watched a devil's darning needle zoom over the water, but her thoughts were centered on the history of the big swamp and its interesting possibilities.

It is just possible, she mused, that the "daughters of the sun" and the enchanted towns on the "elevated

banks of an island" were not tall tales but tag ends
of Indian legends about the first settlers in Okefenokee who left any record of their presence. These
were the Mound Builders.

Where did they come from? Where did they go?
Nobody knows. Mounds, both large and small, are
dotted throughout the swamp. Pottery, tools, and
weapons have been found which are said to be so excellent in workmanship that they could not have been
made by the last Indian swamp dwellers, the Seminoles, or by any of the Creek Nation. One mound
recently excavated yielded the skeleton of a man,
seven feet two inches tall. The Seminoles say the "old
ones" were a race of giants, but they know nothing
now about their origin or end. We have no proof, of
course, that the skeleton man was one of that ancient
race when he walked the earth. He may have been
one of those later Timucuans whose size, strength,
and prowess excited the admiration of the Spaniards
with Narváez and De Soto.

The mounds are there with their superior arti-
facts, as tantalizing illustrations for a story we shall
never know! It may be that invading tribes overcame
the Mound Builders and absorbed the remnants of
them. When the white settlers built their log cabins
around Okefenokee, it was occupied by the Seminoles,
of the Creek Confederacy. The tall Timucuans,
hunted and enslaved by the Spanish at St. Augustine,
declined to a few hundred warriors. The Creeks,
thrusting southeastward a century later, practically
exterminated this once powerful tribe. Creeks is a
translation of the Algonkin Muskoka, or Muskogee,

the name given them by the Indians of the French fur brigades because their land, Alabama and Georgia, was laced with streams. Muskogee is also said to be a word in the Seminole tongue, meaning Many Tribes. Muskogee was one of the dominant linguistic stocks at the period of English colonization and included the Creek, Seminole, Choctaw, and Chickasaw nations.

A Seminole legend relates that before the time of Cortes nearly seven hundred descendants of the Miccosukee Tribe of Mayas left Yucatán, crossed the Gulf of Mexico, followed the coast of North America, and finally landed in southern Georgia, where they joined with the Creek Indians. Later, they disliked the domination of the Creeks and deserted the tribe, being known thereafter as Seminoles, which means Runaways. Some of them settled down contentedly in Okefenokee; but others, early in the eighteenth century, went to Florida to live. The Seminoles who stayed in Okefenokee considered it a safe refuge from the encroaching white men. When the colonists finally took the swampland away from them, a long and bloody war resulted.

Their great chief, Osceola, lived in Okefenokee for about nine years. He was born in Muskogee County in 1800. His mother belonged to the Red Sticks Tribe, a branch of the Creek Indians, and married an English trader named William Powell, with whom she lived for twenty years. Some historians believe that Osceola was the son of William Powell; others dispute this.

Secoffee, another Seminole chief, was known to

the English as Cowkeeper. He had two sons, King Pain and Billy Bowlegs. King Pain was mortally wounded during the Indian wars and was succeeded as chief by Bowlegs, his brother. This same Billy Bowlegs waged such bitter war on the settlers of the Okefenokee region that they built forts on the edge of the swamp in order to protect their lives and property. Some of the fiercest Indian battles were fought on the borders of the swamp country.

General John Floyd, who lived at Fairfield, his plantation on the Satilla River to the north of the swamp, was chosen to lead the army against the Seminoles in their wilderness home and to drive them from Okefenokee. Floyd crossed the big swamp and drove out the Indians, who took refuge in the Everglades. Here they lived fairly peacefully until 1835, when they were ordered to a reservation in Oklahoma. This was the beginning of the second Seminole war, which lasted for seven years.

The Seminoles in Florida have never acknowledged the sovereignty of the United States. They live in the Everglades in the primitive manner of their elders. The State Census of 1935 accounts for less than 450 Seminole Indians. Doubtless there are others, hidden on the snake-infested islands of the Everglades; but the tribe numbers considerably under a thousand people.

The history of this region has gaps that can never be filled. We know nothing of its Indian story between the times of the Mound Builders and the Seminoles. We do not even know just what group of European explorers first discovered Okefenokee. It seems safe to assume that they were Spaniards. A Spanish map dated 1542 shows the swamp surrounded by a cordon of forts. Did these forts ever exist? If so, who built them? What expedition, under whom, was prowling about Okefenokee so early, and building forts for the purpose, so the legend says, of keeping the huge, fierce Indians from coming out to attack them?

Ponce de León is the first white man known to have visited that country; but apparently he did not cross the St. Marys River. In 1528 Narváez was on the Withlacoochee and the Suwannee. According to the report of Alvar Nuñez Cabeza de Vaca, historian of the expedition, Narváez spent several days floundering through "a country very difficult to travel and wonderful to look upon" with very tall trees, lakes, and bogs. The report suggests Okefenokee, or its fringes, at least; especially with the added details about the Indians, who "are large of body and appear at a distance like giants." Cabeza de Vaca reached Mexico in 1536. It is possible that he supplied the authorities with notes and charts which were used for the map of 1542, and that the forts had not been erected but were sketched in to emphasize the necessity of them, if Spaniards hoped to colonize that region successfully.

De Soto may have entered Okefenokee; certainly he was close to it. His lieutenant, Lobillo, whom he dispatched with fifty soldiers to reconnoiter, reported marching over "swampy land where horses could not travel." Legend would have the vicious wild hogs, or "piney woods rooters," of the swamp region as the offspring of De Soto's original thirteen sows, many times removed. By the same mythology, the bands of marsh ponies that roam the coastal islands are declared to be descended from his horses, although not a foal was born on De Soto's march so far as the historians, who went with him, disclose. Horse breeding by an army on the march through strange country seems unlikely at least.

Jean Ribaut, who was sent out from France by Admiral de Coligny, traversed the Tidewater and named some of its rivers. The St. Marys he called the Seine. This is one of the crookedest rivers in the world. It flows more than one hundred and seventy-five miles through white sand country; but as the crow flies the distance is only a scant sixty-five miles from its source on the Georgia-Florida border to the Atlantic.

Ribaut and his colonists were wiped out by Menéndez de Avilés, who took time off for this adventure while he was laying the first stones of St. Augustine. But the cultural influence of early French and Spanish settlers, which still exists in the swamp country, must have come in much later than the days of Ribaut and Menéndez. The Plant Woman met one man of undoubted French descent, even though he had no knowledge of his ancestry, who knew the Latin names of some plants; yet he had never been more than a few miles from his cabin and could scarcely write his name.

Okefenokee being rich in furs, hunters and trappers came from the Georgia settlements, from the Carolinas and Virginia, and from St. Augustine and farther south. Gradually these hardy frontiersmen opened up the swamp wilderness, entering by the Indian trails and waterways, and protecting, through friendship with the Indians, the few settlers who followed in their footsteps. The fur industry of the South never rivaled that of the North, but it was a large part of the economic mainstay of Georgia and South Carolina during the lean years of their early colonization. By the time General Oglethorpe and his colony landed at Savannah, in 1733, the competition for good fur territory was so great that it caused wars between nations and a great deal of dissatisfaction and unrest among the Indians. Pioneer swampers were already poling bales of fox and otter pelts down the green-tinged runs to the outland and sending them on by pack train to the great southern fur depot at Charleston. As late as 1924 hunters and trappers were still finding the swamp a treasurehold of furs. It is claimed that one shipment alone that year was worth about $150,000. Otter and raccoon furnish excellent trapping and hunting. Beavers have practically disappeared. The swamp folk say that the beaver left Okefenokee because of ill treatment by the last swamp Indians.

The legend relates that beavers were often captured and brought up as pets by Indian children. Beaver families resented the kidnaping of their offspring and decided to stop the cruel practice. So the King of the Beaver Tribe went to the Seminole Chief. "Let us make a bargain," he said. "If your people will promise not to steal any more of our infants, we will help you by building dams for you, so that there will be plenty of lakes filled with fish. Also, each year we will send two young Beavers of good family and mentality to grow up and play with your children. But they must be allowed to go home often to see their parents, and they must not be mistreated."

"It is well," the Seminole Chief agreed. And so for a long time the Indian Tribe and the Beaver Tribe lived happily, side by side, helping each other. But after the chief died his son, the new ruler, refused to keep the promise made to the Beavers. "Utter nonsense!" he exclaimed.

A war started between the Indians and the Beavers. Hundreds of Beavers were killed and wounded. Secretly, they prepared to retreat from the swamp which had long been their home. Each night they worked busily, gnawing holes in the dams they had built, so that at an agreed signal they could destroy them, flood the swamp, and drown many of the Indians.

One day, when the Indians had been more cruel than usual, all the Beavers, except those needed to destroy the dams, left the swamp and went to a prepared place of safety. The wisest Beaver of them all was left on guard; as soon as he saw the Indians coming he was to give a warning signal.

Hours passed. The Beavers waited patiently. Suddenly, around the bend of the swamp river, came the Indians, paddling their dugouts quietly up the stream. Whack! Whack! The Beaver on guard slapped the water hard with his broad flat tail before diving to safety. At the signal the dams were destroyed, the waters rushed in torrents down the river, the land was flooded, and many of the Indians were drowned.

Never again, it is said, have the Beavers lived in Okefenokee, but always, since that day, they slap their tails upon the water, as a sign of danger. And, also, ever since then, Okefenokee has been a flooded swamp.

2

After the Treaty of 1670, England and France were technically at peace, but no specific boundary had been established between Florida and Carolina. Disputes arose, and as a means of establishing their supremacy the English located military posts on the south end of Cumberland Island, at the mouth of the St. Marys. By 1720, conditions were so unsettled that King George I, fearing the French or Spanish would claim the Altamaha River section, ordered General Nicholson, Governor of South Carolina, to send one hundred soldiers to build a fort near the junction of the Oconee and Ocmulgee rivers, to be called Fort King George. The soldiers rebelled and Nicholson's attempt was a failure. But the danger to British interests in the Altamaha region increased, and it was the political motive for granting the Georgia charter to Oglethorpe and for the English plantings at Savannah, Ebenezer, Darien, and Frederica.

During these fifty years the Spanish were very active in their attempts to colonize Florida. They built the famous Kings Road from St. Augustine to Coleraine on the coast, and established trading posts along the way. It was on this route, years later—in 1796—beneath a giant water oak near the swamp, that representatives of the United States signed the treaty of peace with the Creek Confederacy. A monument to commemorate this event has been erected on the spot by the Waycross Chapter of the Daughters of the American Revolution.

Spain ceded Florida to Great Britain in 1763 in exchange for Cuba. Four years later Dr. Andrew Turnbull settled New Smyrna, fronting on Mosquito Lagoon, the northern bayou of Indian River. He was given a grant of sixty thousand acres by the British Government and colonized it with wild mountaineers from southern Greece, Italian convicts, and peasants of mixed Catalonian, Moorish, and Spanish blood from the Balearic Islands. Dr. Turnbull laid out great plantations for growing sugar cane and indigo, but the struggle to subdue the tropical wilderness and the hostile Indians was too much for the new colony. In 1777 the few who had remained moved to St. Augustine. Perhaps some adventurous son of Greece traveled farther north, for an old Greek coin has been found recently on one of the islands in Okefenokee.

During the various wars the swamp was refuge for deserters and runaway slaves. There was food in plenty and good water. The swamp water, as well as that of the St. Marys River, is well liked by all the swamp folk. Some of them used to sell water from the river to captains of sailing vessels for about a cent a gallon.

3

The Indians gave the first settlers in the Okefenokee region corn, beans, pumpkins, melons, and fruits and taught them how to plant and care for them. They showed them how to make oil from walnuts, pecans, and other nuts, crushing and boiling them and preserving the oil in earthen jars. A writer of the time claims that this oil was "clear as butter and of good taste."

But soon dissension arose between the Indians and the settlers of the swamp and Suwannee country. The militia were called out, which enraged the Indians: they felt that they were only fighting for their homes, for the land that had always belonged to Seminoles. Bloody raids followed, one of which is famed in local history as Wilde's Massacre. Troops were camped on Kettle Creek, trying vainly to drive the last of the Seminoles from Okefenokee. Wilde, an Englishman who lived near by, went to the swamp one morning to collect ash wood, and saw signs of Indians. His wife, alarmed for the safety of her children, implored him to leave their cabin and seek refuge in Wilkinson settlement, but he refused.

That night, as Mrs. Wilde cooked their supper over the open fire in the yard, she heard the war whoops of the Seminoles, but it was too late then to fly to safety. The Indians attacked at dawn. Six of the Wilde family were killed, the baby being murdered with a lightwood knot buried in its head. Four of the children hid in the swamp and eventually made their way to a neighbor's house. The cabin was burned, and soldiers arriving hours later buried the bodies near a large tree that still stands to mark the graves. The city of Waycross is built near the scene of this tragedy.

After the Seminoles were driven into Florida, nothing of special interest occurred in the Okefenokee region until an engineer, Colonel R. L. Hunter, was employed by the State of Georgia to ascertain if the swamp could be drained. His survey, it is claimed, cost the state over $3,000. The years passed with nothing done, until in 1875 the Atlanta *Constitution*, in co-operation with the State Geological Survey, systematically explored much of the big swamp. Timber specimens were sent to the Paris Exposition, and a published list of them is apparently the first authentic botanical information ever to be printed about that region.

Most of Okefenokee remained the property of the State of Georgia until 1889. Many of the swamp folk, however, lived on the public lands and considered them their own by right of inheritance. But in 1890 Georgia sold her remaining interest in the region for 26½ cents per acre to the Suwannee Canal Company, headed by Captain Henry Jackson, an enterprising visionary. In 1891 Jackson began to cut the swamp timber. He dug one canal from the St. Marys River to the edge of Okefenokee, and another toward the middle of the swamp. He intended to float logs and eventually to drain the swamp through these canals. But Okefenokee could not be drained of its primeval waters, and Jackson's company suspended operations. The unlucky venture is said to have cost nearly a million dollars, and the canal is still called Jackson's Folly. The Hebard Cypress Company began logging there in 1908. They laid thirty-five miles of track to transport their lumber from the heart of the swamp to the railroad; but it seems that "earth trembling" had the better of them, too! Today most of their holdings are included in the three hundred thousand acres of Okefenokee that the United States Biological Survey secured in 1936 as a sanctuary for all forms of wild life. John Hopkins, who guided the Survey's scientific observers on their explorations of the swamp, is now Superintendent in Charge of the Okefenokee Wildlife Refuge. He has engaged some of his old cronies, the best guides in the swamp, to patrol the Reserve, and, more important still, to educate the folk about the great need for game protection. The swampers would be suspicious if told by an outlander that indiscriminate killing must cease: they listen to one of their own people, born and bred to hunting. So, under supervision, the people of Okefenokee are developing a genuine interest in the Survey's purpose.

The journey to the St. Marys had opened up new lanes of travel and botanical research to the Plant Woman. Yet one run, one prairie, one thick cypress bay looked so much like another and "here" seemed only a mirror of "there" with no signs, which she could detect, to direct a traveler. She watched Freeman poling through the maze with perfect confidence, and asked him if he had ever been lost. Yes, it seemed he had been, once. Years ago. He was a young man then, only just married to Manthy. He remembered it well. It wasn't a thing a man could forget—

such "ventures in dark places!" Okefenokee had put her mood of fear on him, then. He could recall that, too. It was with him again while he talked.

CHAPTER THREE

Adventures in Dark Places

THE gum and cypress trees were dense around him, and all the swamp was covered with gloom. A chill wind rose from the water and gray squirrels sped homeward over the matted undergrowth. "Ye an' me hain't lost," Freeman Carter told the push-pole in his hand, "we is jest misplaced." Yet he shivered as though a hant had touched him with its ghostly fingers, for night was near and he was alone in a depth of the swamp where he had never been before.

"Soon be dark as pitch, an' we-uns better find a likely spot to roost." He spoke aloud, talking to the familiar things about him, as all swampers do. "Come calm o' day, we-uns'll take our bearin's off the sun an' light for home." He thought a bit. "Iffen we can find hit," he added gravely, remembering settlers who had entered the big swamp never to return, and tales of bleached bones found months later, picked clean by scavengers, and stories about other men who had disappeared without a trace. "Recken as how they-uns was plumb keerless," he consoled himself.

Early that morning he had scared a wild black bull from its bed among the low palmettos. It was a prize that carried no man's mark, and he followed it deeper and deeper into the heart of the swamp, hoping to turn it homeward. In late afternoon a thin, wispy mist rose from the steamy morass and the bull swam across the run and disappeared into the fog. Since then he had searched in vain for a familiar landmark, such as an osprey's nest or a buzzard's roost, to guide him.

He tried one channel after another, looking for a blazed trail, and found none. Near nightfall, he realized he was hopelessly lost. Panic swept over him like a great black cloud. On the deep water of the lake, fog lay thick and smothery, like a feather bed, and he hugged the shores of the cypress bay, hoping to find an open run. Again and again, until his voice was only a croak, he had given the deep, booming hoot of the deer owl—a distress signal of the swampers when far from home—but, although he knew it must have carried for miles, only the echoes had an-

swered. Exhausted, he crouched in the bottom of the
boat to rest, pulling his shabby coat around him to
keep out the chill. Night birds flew around his head
with piercing squeaks. The boat drifted until branches
from overhanging bushes scraped its side. Something
cold and wet and clinging touched his face and he
shrieked aloud in terror, pushing it away with desperate hands. Frantically he poled out into deeper
water, lest a cottonmouth drop from a limb into
the boat.

Half blind with fear, Freeman followed the drift
of the current. He had heard somewhere that drifting
objects emerge eventually in the waters of the Suwannee. Once he reached the river, he would be safe. On
and on he drifted, losing track of time, until at last he
discovered that he was in a twisting waterway. The
low boat slipped under the drooping branches of a
buttonbush like a swimming rabbit, with the man
flat in the bottom, and white blossoms from the bush
scattered petals on his hat. The run widened slightly
on the other side of the barrier and the fog was thin-
ner, even though a weird green twilight mist tinged
everything and made it seem unreal. Pulling himself
together, he poled along with the current, a-studyin'
on what he knew about the swamp. "Hit's nary
changed a-tall since a thousand years ago," he considered. "Hit's like nothin' else in the world. Nary
person knows a-tall how hit come to be, 'pears like."
The great marsh was a place of myth and mystery,
and he feared it, even though it so fascinated him
that he returned to it, day after day, even without
cause, and was unhappy when away. "Jest like a rat-

tler a-drawin' down a bird," he marveled, and, in spite of his fear, was pleased at his imagining.

But now the swamp seemed cold and menacing, filled with lurking horrors. It was the time between day and night when nearly all the world is still. A sheer wall of buttressed trunks rose some eighty feet into the air on both sides of the narrow channel. The bay was beautiful in its riot of lush foliage, but it was also sinister. Evil seemed to exude from its luxuriance. "Must be tuk with a franzy spell," Freeman thought, as for the first time in his life it appeared to him that the prolific growth was unhealthy—the greens too green—the green of living things that feed upon death and destruction. All around were flowers whose scent was sweet and sickish, blooming palely in the festering humidity of the dusky marsh. Strangling vines and clinging plants choked the trees to which they clung. And well he knew that in the humid hollows of the forest floor were hidden poisonous things that creep and crawl, and other bolder poisonous things lay in coils and folds across the cypress knees.

The channel wound around decaying logs and rotting stumps. Dimly, through the mist, Freeman saw a lone tree standing in a little clearing, like a lighthouse on an island. He poled toward it through the cypress knees until the water shallowed and he stepped out on hammocks of black muck. He tied the boat securely to a sapling and moved warily toward firmer ground. "Trembling earth, the Seminoles called it," he told the twelve-gauge shotgun in his hand, "an' hit was a plumb fitten name," he added as he saw the huge trees quiver and shake at his tread.

Before him a little path opened, flat-trodden by the feet of animals coming to drink the brown water. He followed it through a tall stand of maiden cane and skirted a quagmire surrounded by pale yellow cannas and deep blue iris. He made a wide circuit of the treacherous pool, knowing how such places dragged cattle, and even men, down into bottomless depths. Only last year a hunter from the outland was sucked down, "slow an' deliberate," while his friend looked on, powerless to help. Freeman's lips were dry, just thinking about it, and he moistened them with his tongue. "Must fret him powerful." He brushed his hand across his eyes and shook such thoughts from him.

On the other side of the pool was a dense thicket of gallberry and hurrah bushes. It was hours since he had eaten. Even in a realm of hants and specters a fleshly man needs food. Freeman pulled himself together and looked around for game. He circled the thicket, hoping to scare up a marsh rabbit, and discovered that blue scoggins, or herons, were late-nesting in the bushes five or six feet above the water. One bird, startled by his passing, flew out with a loud squawk, and he shot quickly, for he knew that it might be his last chance for supper. He pushed into the thicket, looking for new-laid eggs, but the few he found were nearly hatched.

He retraced his steps to where the heron had fallen. As he straightened, with the bird in his hand, the sense of danger, which familiarity with swamp and wilderness develops in its people, warned him, and he stopped dead still. Always, from dawn to dawn, the swamp folk must be on guard—on guard against the things they seldom see, for fear that when they see them it will be too late. There had been no sound, only the slightest darkening of a shadow on the ground; he sensed something there rather than heard it. But his nostrils also were warning him now:

the smell of fish was strong, but another odor was mingled with it. His keen eyes searched the shadows, and sweat beaded his forehead and his throat went dry; he breathed with his mouth wide open to avoid making a sound. All around him were the thick, loathsome bodies of snakes—deadly cottonmouths and diamondbacks—congregated there to feed on the fish dropped by the nesting herons. Two—four—six—thirteen—he counted in the dim light, and how many more were coiled in the long grass, and hidden among the bushes, he had no way of knowing. The air was dank and nauseating from the musty stench of the gorging reptiles, twined and twisted together as they writhed over the fish. One large female snake was coiled near his boot, with her companion stretched beside her, his head laid protectingly across her body. Freeman had almost stepped on them. Sluggish though they are by nature, cottonmouth moccasins strike, he knew, at the slightest motion. The sharp fangs would slash his cowhide brogan like a knife cutting through butter. Death would follow in a few hours: a horrible death with one convulsion after another, until his bloated body lay quiet near the lonely trail. Through his mind flashed a picture, and he wondered how long it would be before the buzzards, always circling lazily beneath the burning sky, would find courage to descend and ring his carcass in; and he saw his bones, months later, lying white against the sear brown grass of winter.

The snake hissed and drew back its broad, wicked head. Glittering eyes, green-slitted and cold as ice, glared straight into his face. "A ole she-un," the man said dully, never realizing that he spoke aloud. "Hain't no markin's on hits sides." The wide mouth yawned open, showing the cottony white lining which gives the snake its name. The head flashed forward. Swift as thought, he threw the limp bird in his hand straight at it. The vicious force of the snake's darting blow knocked the bird far to one side; but, even in the dusk, the shuddering man thought he could see the greenish yellow venom oozing in long streaks down the silky blue feathers. Before the snake could strike again he clubbed it savagely with his gun, then ground the evil head to pulp beneath his heavy boot. For a few seconds he was safe. The old "she-un's" lunge had rolled her mate to one side, farther along the path, where it barred his way. Shaken and sick though he was, he went methodically about killing it.

Night had closed in when Freeman reached the shelter of the big tree. Wet mist rose from the water and floated, white and curling, over shore and forest. Okefenokee stirred gently, then shook herself and awoke. The throaty cries of hoot owls assailed him from every tree and little "scrich" owls cried from every branch. "Jest feed time for them hootin' critters," he assured himself and pulled moss from the tree to make his bed. He sat with his back against the trunk, listening to the monotonous grunt of the pig-frog and, so listening, tired from the long day, he fell asleep.

A sound aroused him. Bullbats swept past, with their shivering notes, and moths struck his face. A fox barked shrilly for its mate. A prowling wildcat missed its prey and screamed with rage. The hair on the back of his neck rose in bristles and he held his breath, listening in an agony of fear. Perspiration, in spite of the chill night wind, ran down his face and body in little streams. From the black shadow of a bush two small gleaming eyes gazed steadily at him and he prayed lustily that it might not be a diamond-back rattlesnake, lured to him by the odor on his boots of the fish he had trodden. Unwinking, the eyes appeared to watch him; but, when it seemed that he could bear no more, they vanished suddenly from sight. "Manthy," he cried aloud, like a child calling for its mother.

Something big and black and heavy crashed through the underbrush. With a yell of utter panic the man ran, how far he did not know, until a trailing vine tripped him with its clutching tendrils and he fell face down in the black muck. The fall shook him into reason. He stood up and groped his way back to the tree, outlined against the sky. His jaws set stiffly and sweat dried on his body as he again faced the unfriendly darkness. The very trees seemed to close in on him as he walked, crouching like panthers ready to crush him beneath their velvet paws. From far off in the swamp came sounds that seemed to him unearthly and chilled his blood. Shapes of terror drew closer and closer, so that he did not dare to look behind. Greenish lights flickered here and there in the forest, lights that rose and fell. Even in his fear, the trained woodsman speculated on their origin.

Hours later a pale moon peered over the tips of the hammock and sent long shadows wavering across the clearing. There was no wind now, but the shadows seemed to swirl as though alive. In the branches above him a limpkin cried, making the night more hideous with its wailing. The moon, rising higher, darted gleams of light across the hidden islands of the swamp and woke a chuck-will's-widow, whose cry is the loneliest sound in the world. *"Whip-poor-will! Whip-pur-will! Whip-p-ee-er-wi-ill!"*—far off and hopeless. "Shet yer mouth," Freeman screamed to the mourning bird; and, as though frightened by his voice, it fell silent. Then, timidly, *"Whip!"* and in a few seconds "*Whip-pur*," and then in quick succession "*Whip! Whip! Whip-eer*"—and triumphantly, but soft and low—"*Whip . . . pur . . . wi . . . ill!*" From the bay a bull gator roared challenge and another answered. There were other sounds, which he

had never heard from any animal or bird that he knew, and shapes made of shadow moved in the moonglow. "Hants," his frozen lips framed the word. No man could protect himself against these. He held his hands over his ears and crouched lower still in his bed of moss and covered up his head.

Hours passed. At last dawn painted its first silver over the lonely swamp. Freeman sat up, amazed to find that he was still alive. But when he found 't was so, he picked up his gun, useless during the night— for what gun is proof against hants?—and started off toward the run. Then he decided to hitch up to the first branch of the big pine and climb high enough to spot a familiar landmark. "Mayhap," he thought, "we-uns kin git our bearin' without need for spuddin' aroun'." From a height of fifty feet he looked down upon the marsh, and through the breaks in the trees saw nothing but a maze of tiny channels cutting the tangle of underbrush and cypresses that formed the bays. "We-uns kin never," he declared hopelessly. Then he turned around—and shouted for joy. He pulled off his hat and said solemnly, "We-uns thank you kindly, Lord!" Less than a hundred yards ahead the run opened into a wide prairie dotted with wooded islets and small gator holes. Deer were feeding on the succulent roots beneath the water, and a black bear ambled down the banks of the near-by Suwannee, to fish for its breakfast. "I'm a-hongry, too," Freeman said.

He slid to the ground in haste. "Mortal glad I am to see yon prairie," he told the push-pole as he shoved off into the stream. "Right proud us'll be to see our homesite. Belike Manthy'll be clean bereft, we-uns havin' stayed so long on our ventures." The boat slid over a big log, stuck in a shallow black slough, and then darted forward, free, into the open prairie. The man's heart was so light that his voice rose blithely in his favorite song, "Fair Ellender." And all the rice birds, swaying on the waving maiden cane, tilted their black heads and sang with him as he told how she rode through forest and town, to attend the wedding of her faithless lover:

> She dressed herself in scarlet red,
> Her maidens, they dressed in green:
> An' every town that they rode through
> They took her to be a queen.

Now, years later, Freeman, the best guide in the swamp, poled slowly through a flower-garlanded patch of sun. "Okefenokee's a purty place." But one couldn't afford to be keerless. That day, long ago, when he went plunging after the bull, he should have recorded a landmark or two in his mind at the same time. He had trained his sons not to take chances. Obadiah, he thought, was more cautious and efficient at twenty than his father had been at the same age. The other boys—Absalom, who was fourteen, and Silas, who was ten—were smart boogers too. They would be going out some night soon to prove their manhood by camping in the wilderness, " 'midst b'ars an' gators an' hants that float an' scrich. The two of 'em togither, 'cause no swamper, boy or man grown, will spend a night alone in the swamp."

"I wish they'd take me with them!" said the Plant Woman, excited by the idea.

Freeman thought they might, if she made her request tactfully. Truly there was nothing he-uns of any age enjoyed more than showin' off afore a wom-ern—sich foolish! But he couldn't say anything about it, really. It was the boys' business.

CHAPTER FOUR

Cannibals of the Swamp

"Time ye larned to keer for yerselves," Freeman said to Absalom and Silas after the midday meal a few days later. "Can't stay tied to yer maw's apron strings all yer life." He glanced at the Plant Woman, with a twinkle in his eyes. "Swamp young-uns has to larn right early to live off the land, an' to hold steady when they're skeert," he said. "Mayhap ye

64

might git a gator, an' then ye'd have some gator teeth to be carved into flower ornaments for the fowkses in the outland. But no poachin' on gov'ment land, mind, lessen ye be compelled for food. We-uns be a law-abidin' lot."

Late in the afternoon the boys went to a tiny unnamed island and started to clear a campsite as their father had taught them.

"This here looks a likely spot." Absalom used the brush hook vigorously. "Look right smart for sarpents, Silas. Pappy says rattlers are right partial to huckleberry bushes."

Silas brushed the blond thatch of hair from his eyes and grinned at his brother. "Hain't no sarpents here, Ab. I can smell 'em way off. Rattlers smell jest like ripe watermelons an' ole cottonmouths smell stronger, all musty like."

The camp took shape rapidly. Silas lighted a small fire of fatwood splinters that snapped and crackled cheerily between the two long flat stones of the hearth. A thicket of hardwood ringed in the camp and gave the spot a homelike atmosphere. The wide trunk of a big gum made an ideal back rest while eating. For sleeping quarters, a few poles were stuck into the soft ground and roofed with palmetto thatch; under this shelter, on a platform of crossed poles, the boys spread beds of Spanish moss for themselves and the Plant Woman and covered them with some old hand-pieced quilts, lent by Manthy. After a supper of broiled marsh rabbit, which Absalom shot as it swam across the run, they built up a strong smudge to keep away the sand flies, and the boys stretched out at their ease.

The frogs were choiring to the night in a bog beside the small isle. The Plant Woman, who could never tire of these diversified and persistent singers, took her flashlight and crept down to the bog's edge.

Among the choristers the leopard frogs were close by, evidently, for the flashlight disclosed, first, a number of the females of that species sitting placidly on floating leaves near the bank and listening to the music made in their honor. Now and then they seemed a bit bored with the role of audience—only the males sing—and took a little nourishment, snapping down low-flying aquatic insects. Then the flash picked out the singing males. They were thick in the rank marsh grass. When silence fell for a moment, one would puff out his yellow throat and start his staccato theme. Immediately, the chorus would join in until hundreds of voices poured upward into the night and echoes came from far off. Occasionally a knight-errant lost the time beat of the music, but he warbled valiantly notwithstanding. On and on, with tireless ecstasy, the leopard frogs sang the serenade to their ladyloves.

Okefenokee is a frog lover's paradise. Each kind of frog has a different note, and it takes a trained herpetologist to distinguish between them. The southern frog has a voice out of all proportion to his size and roars right lustily, blowing up a sac beneath his chin until it seems that no frog in the world could possibly swell to such a size. There is one frog that sounds like dozens of hammers striking against an empty barrel, and the natives call him the "smith."

According to many of the swamp folk the red-headed scorpion, one of the seven species of lizards found in Okefenokee, barks like a dog and is deadly poisonous. Neither statement is true. But since the swampers believe the creature to be poisonous they hunt it down and destroy it wherever they find it. It lives commonly in the hammocks on old, half-rotted logs. The race nag (six-lined lizard), the ground lizard, and the orange-tailed skink are all found in the swamp in numbers, but are not so well known as the chameleon, whose courting the swamp folk view with delight. This lizard wears a leaf-green coat with a white waistcoat; during the mating season the male glides up to the female, poised among the green shrubs, and bows solemnly before her for two or three minutes, expanding to the fullest his thin throat fan of brilliant rose pink. The male fence lizard, when courting, displays his radiant blue and black under-parts by rising high on his front limbs and then bobbing quickly up and down.

Suddenly another melody burst upon the night air. From afar in the swamp the three islanders heard a human voice raised in song:

Once there was a little ship an' she sailed upon the sea,
An' she went by the name of the *Mary Golden Tree,*
An' she sailed upon the lone and the lonesome low
An' she sailed upon the lonesome sea.

"Cap'n Beamy, sure for sartin." Absalom sat up with a jerk. "Must be goin' after gators. Mayhap he'd take we-uns along." He put his hands to his mouth and gave the ringing call of the swamp folk. A lusty hail answered him, and in a few minutes old Captain Beamy poled through the run and beached his boat upon the sandy shore.

He squinted at the two boys sitting in the light of the campfire, greeted the Plant Woman, then looked around for Freeman. "Yer Pappy tossed ye out alone, eh? Well, 'spect ye have to larn sometime. Yerse." He sat down and pulled his old pipe from his pocket. The "Cap'n" was such by courtesy only, but no one in the swamp country ever called him anything else. He had traded up and down the coast for years, catching rattlesnakes and gators for their hides, and many was the fine story he could tell.

"Goin' after gators, Cap'n?" Silas leaned forward eagerly. "Pappy's right anxious to git some teeth for carvin' for the outlanders. What say we-uns take the teeth an' ye take the hides, an' we team up, come moondown?"

"Four, five hours till moondown. Hain't no use to hunt gators iffen the moon be up."

"How many gators ye kotched in a night, Cap'n?" Absalom asked.

"Biggest catch I ever got was forty. But that was years ago, an' gators was thick as flies on a honeypot. Why, when I fust come into the swamp they was so thick ye could walk across the prairies on their backs. Nuvver see so many elsewhere. An' big! An' bad, too, as they can be! Why, I've heerd tell as how they used to foller hunters' boats an' try to smash 'em with their tails, to git the huntin' dogs outen 'em. Yerse.

An' any gator got hurt, the rest piled on him an' picked him clean. Cannibals, they be."

"What's cannibals, Cap'n?" Young Silas leaned forward, eager not to miss a word.

"A cannibal is any kind of a animal that ets up hits own kind. Like ole bull gators eatin' their young, an' piney woods rooters eatin' their babies, an' snakeses eatin' other snakeses, an' so on. That ole he king snake as belongs to Snake Woman of Cowhouse, he's a cannibal. He kills rattlers an' eats 'em too, an' other kinds of snakeses. Lotsa animals be cannibals."

"Did ye ever see gators eatin' other gators, Cap'n?" Absalom asked.

"Sartin did. Hain't ye ever heerd about the gator battle down the river? Ole Georgia paper, printed in Savannah, wrote up news of the battle; so hit's gospel truth, as ye can tell. Well, it 'pears everybody says as how the king of the gators as lived here in Okefenokee, an' the king of the gators as lived downriver in Floridy, got fightin' with each other, an' nuther would give in. Seems like they has some way of talkin' back an' forth. An' they challenged each other with all kinds of truckish tricks, like standin' on their heads with their tails up agin a tree, with all the other gators lookin' on, an' sich foolish.

"After nigh on to three months they was still fightin' an' fightin'. But the king of the Okefenokee gators he got tired of hit and *de*clared war. An' he and his warriors, twenty thousand strong, swum down the river. But they met the king of the river gators comin' up with his troops, nigh about twenty thousand strong, an' the battle begun. They stood up

on their tails an' fit; they bellowed so loud ye could
hear 'em fifty miles off; their jaws snapped till they
sounded like cypress trees a-fallin'. More than a thousand acres was a-kivered with the dead an' the dyin'.
An' then the gators turned cannibals, an' et an' et till
they could et no more. That I seed with my own eyes.
An' for months an' years after, here in the swamp,
an' down the river, ye could hardly get a hide that
was whole—some had arms off, an' some had no legs
or tails."

Silas let his breath out with a loud whistle.
"Hain't that somethin'?"

2

The night was velvet black. The Cap'n poled
carefully up the run. Fish splashed in the shallows and
the dank smell of crushed reeds and grasses rose on
the air as the boat pushed through acres of them.
Then the Cap'n left Absalom to pole the boat, and
pulled on his old felt hat. Fastened to the front was a
miner's lamp with a reflecting mirror. Its powerful
beam, aided by the Plant Woman's flashlight, made
a flood of light to pierce the dark waters of the run
and the near-by gator holes, but their owners were
not at home.

The boat slid out of the run into a tiny lake bor-
dered by dense hardwood thickets and blueberry
bushes, under which gators love to lie. "Waitin' for
their dinners to float to 'em," the Cap'n explained.
He kept up a running fire of comment, interrupted
by occasional remarks from Absalom. Silas was fas-

cinated by the grotesque shadows the man's body cast, as the light swept back and forth. He whispered to the Plant Woman, drawing her attention to the Cap'n as reflected on the night waters. He was sometimes a savage black bear, a-huntin', then a big ole giant, such as Silas had heard lived on Bugaboo Island, an' agin he was long an' slim, like a sliver. The night was very still; not even a chuck-will's-widow called. They poled one mile, two miles, upstream.

Suddenly the Cap'n held his hand back for the heavy spear that he used in night hunting. The others looked steadily into the circle of light on the water. A muttered order and the boat was shoved forward, inch by inch. The Cap'n raised the spear. And now they could see the quarry plainly, his eye mounds above the water, and his feet outlined below.

It is not an easy thing to spear a gator. Except for his nostrils and eyes, he is almost completely submerged and his back is covered with an armor of bony plates which, in the mature animal, are almost impenetrable. The trick is to pierce his side, where the armor plates join the soft skin of the belly.

The Cap'n struck. The water was churned into foam. The gator's lashing tail hit the boat, knocking out a section of it—fortunately above the water line —as though it were made of cardboard. Again and again the gator leaped clear of the water, snapping its jaws and grunting in rage. Then Absalom slipped a rope noose over the wide, blunt head, pulled it tight, and wound the other end around a small homemade winch fastened to the boat. The gator struggled desperately, tearing aquatic plants loose from the bot-

tom of the shallows. The Cap'n waited till the beast
was tired, then wound up the winch. He slipped a
second noose around the thick, wicked tail, pulled the
rope taut, and hoisted his catch aboard. It was an
old bull over twelve feet long.

3

Among all the wild life in Okefenokee, with
their various habits and customs, the big alligators
are probably the most interesting. The swamp is undoubtedly the best place to find these armored sauri-
ans; they reach a greater length there than elsewhere
in America. It is an excellent place for scientists and
other interested individuals to study their life habits.

On warm spring evenings the swamp country
rings with the hollow, booming bellow of the big
bulls, who trumpet their love songs from half-submerged logs along the winding Suwannee, or from
the shelter of the maiden cane that covers the prairies.
According to various old chroniclers, the early settlers could scarcely sleep at night, anywhere in the
swamp country, because of the horrible din made by
the wild beasts. The wolf, perhaps, has vanished. Some
people say the "painters," or pumas, are no longer
found in Okefenokee, but hunters deny this. The
wildcats and black bears are still plentiful. And the
alligators still sing as loudly and as terrifyingly as ever.

Today, as of old, there are numerous authentic
cases of gators' attacking human beings. To come deliberately within reach of their jaws, or wicked lashing tails, is folly. William Bartram, in his journey

through the South, was attacked in his boat by huge alligators. Other reliable witnesses testify to the fact that the reptiles pull their prey beneath the water and drown it, or kill it with a slap of the tail.

In the early days of America the settlers had good opportunities for observing the reactions of alligators to other animals, more so than today, when all wild life is to some extent depleted. Old bull gators are formidable-looking monsters, especially when seen in the half-light of dawn or of dusk, as they glide through the brown water.

Sir Charles Lyell, the English geologist, visited a naturalist at Darien, Georgia, and in his notes regarding the alligators of the coastal lowlands he wrote:

In the summer of 1845 he [Mr. Couper, his host] saw a shoal of porpoises coming up to that part of the Altamaha where the fresh and salt water meet . . . the favorite fishing ground of the alligators. . . . Here were seen about fifty alligators, each with head and neck raised above the water, looking down the stream at their enemies [porpoises], before whom they had fled, terror-stricken, and expecting an attack. The porpoises, no more than a dozen in number, moved on in two ranks, and were evidently complete masters of the field. So powerful are they that they have been known to chase a large alligator to the bank, and putting their snouts lightly under his belly, toss him ashore.

Alligators do occasionally swim down tidal rivers, and undoubtedly they meet porpoises in their wanderings. But whether or not porpoises make war in this manner is apparently an unanswerable question today.

Most of the alligators in Okefenokee are from six

to ten feet long; the greatest length known appears to be about sixteen feet. Some of them are captured with live bait, such as a small shote, tied to a rope and thrown overboard from a boat. Some hunters use guns; but the quarry is likely to be lost, and a crippled gator is the prey of all his relatives.

The female alligator makes her nest near water, in some open spot where the sun can shine down warmly through the trees. She digs a shallow hole in the sand, or earth, and deposits twenty, thirty, or even more, dull white eggs, then covers them carefully with dead leaves, sticks, and trash until she has made a mound about three feet high and twice that in diameter. The eggs are nearly four inches long and as big around as a hen's egg; the young six-inch gators lie in them, coiled like worms. The sun performs the work of incubation, and by the time the cool days of autumn have come the young are hatched and well able to care for themselves. Alligators feed on fish, snakes, frogs, small birds, raccoons, and sometimes baby gators and wounded adults. Dogs and hogs are favorite food and are quickly snapped up if they are foolish enough to enter waters where alligators abound, or to come close enough to the brink so that the gator can strike them into the water with his tail. Once caught in those powerful jaws, even large dogs have no chance of escape.

Like other reptiles, an alligator prefers hot weather, and although none of the swamp animals go into complete hibernation, in wintertime the snakes and the alligators are seen only on warm days.

Alligators breathe equally well on land and in

water. They make caves below the surface, generally three or more feet wide and from six to fifteen feet deep. Prey caught in the water is pulled into these caves—if the beasts are not hungry enough to devour it immediately—and stored. There it softens and provides food in wet weather or on cold days.

The terrapin of Okefenokee is not a cannibal. Its moral weakness is laziness. The "hard-backed cooter," as the swampers call it, is often seen sunning itself on logs above the water. During the summer months, in common with other swamp turtles, it deposits its eggs in the sandy banks of the Suwannee. But the hard-backed cooter is too indolent to dig even a small hole in the soft sand to make its own nest. It burrows into the mass of leaves and muck piled up by the alligators and lays its eggs there. Another turtle, the industrious and hospitable gopher, digs large burrows and acts as host to lizards, toads, frogs, spiders, rabbits, gray fox, skunks, and snakes, including the king snake and the large indigo snake. Many of these are only temporary guests, but a few others, such as the gopher frog, apparently move in permanently.

One of the most dangerous cannibals in the swamp country is the wild hog, or piney woods rooter. It is the deadliest enemy of the diamondback rattle-snake, which it tears to bits and eats. This animal's thick hide makes it impervious to any snake's fangs.

Rooters are huge, grayish creatures, utterly wild and savage, that haunt the fastnesses of the moss-draped swamp thickets, sallying forth to war on young lambs, deer, dogs, or any other animals they consider worth eating; sometimes they even eat their own litter. For tidbits they dig up and eat the roots of young pines, which explains their local name. These pirates of the pinelands are run down with dogs trained for that purpose. The hunters usually trail the dogs in companies of twos and threes. Few men, even though armed, care to face one of these ruthless killers alone. By the time the hunter has come within range, more often than not he will see the rooter's gleaming tusks stained scarlet with the blood of the dog it has gored. Like demons from the nether world, the old boars turn at bay, covered from head to foot with thick, stiff gray bristles; their small, vicious eyes gleam red in the half gloom of the un-derbrush, and they champ their foam-flecked jaws and toss their heavy heads. With one thrust the boar, whose four curved tusks are as sharp as daggers and may be five or even six inches long, can deliver a deathblow.

Piney woods rooters as a rule roam the forests in small groups, supposedly families; but during the cold days of winter, or in times of hunger or danger, they run in packs. The swamp folk believe the rooters to be descended from the first pigs brought into Florida by the early Spanish settlers, and this is generally the opinion of scientists. Through the centuries they have reverted to their wild ancestors. Probably even their frames have changed. At any rate, the rooters have longer noses and more massive heads and shoulders than the razorbacks, which were domestic swine much more recently. The razorback, running half wild in the piney woods, is also dangerous, but is not to be compared with the real piney woods rooter. Razorbacks are sometimes captured and penned by swamp folk; but nobody would take that chance with rooters!

CHAPTER FIVE

Snake Woman of Cowhouse

I T was the beginning of a midsummer evening. Dusk filtered into the clearing and blurred the outlines of the low matted growth of swamp oak, cypress, and young pine that hemmed it in. Snake Woman had lived here in the old log cabin for more than sixty years. She had outlasted two husbands, ten sons, plagues of grasshoppers, numerous droughts, forest fires, and all the other happenings of life and death since her arrival on Cowhouse Island as a bride of seventeen.

Light still shone dimly above the swamp to the west of the stump lot. Here and there a bald cypress reared its shaggy head against the sky, while the plowed fields were encircled with gray wisps of twilight. On the split-rail fence at the foot of the tiny garden stretched drying hides of gators and diamondbacks—fair money they would bring in the outland. Beyond the fence was the prairie, flanked on both sides by dense bays of stately cypresses. It reached clear to the great stand of slash pine where blueberries grew and cattle pastured, and men, who were hunted, hid.

Supper was over and the dishes were done. The Plant Woman sat sidewise on the doorsill and hugged her knees. In this pose she could see into the kitchen, where the Snake Woman was preparing a dish for her beloved pet snake. Cooking King's supper was his mistress's favorite task, and she hummed contentedly as she went about it. The sound of her smothered song was thin and nasal: it suggested the feeble twanging of a thin tight wire.

She poured milk into an old copper vessel and set it to heat over the fire. There was no cookstove in the house—"dum fureen contraption," she called it, and continued to cook with the old crane and cast-iron kettles, and the occasional copper pots of this or that sort, which were relics of olden days. The milk heated to her satisfaction, and the King's taste, she poured it into a bowl, walked briskly past her guest and across the porch, and attempted a whistle—so hard to do when you have no teeth. But her faint lisping note was enough. The slim black shape that slithered from beneath the cellarless cabin knew the

call well. She set the dish of lukewarm milk on the
ground. King rippled up to it and partly over the
edge and drank to the last drop. The Snake Woman
picked up the glittering coils with a toilworn, gentle
hand. Crooning tender words, she padded over the
ground to the swing. *Squeak, squeak-k-k* went the old

swing as she swayed placidly to and fro, giving herself an extra push occasionally with one horny, bare
foot. The long snake slept peacefully, draped across
her lap, its white rings catching and holding the last
of the evening light.

It was all so peaceful and quiet—New York
seemed very far away. The Plant Woman found it
good to sit there in silence, letting the dusk thicken
about her and draw her into it. Time seemed not to
exist; it passed without speech, without awareness
sharp enough to be called thought, while she leaned
her head back against the door jamb, her eyes half

closed. Dreamily she gazed at the old woman and the big snake in the swing. What a painting that would make, she thought. Though bent by years, trouble, and hard work, her face creased by hundreds of grimed-in, wrinkled lines, the Snake Woman's deep-set blue eyes shone with a spirit as fierce and unbeaten as that which gleamed in the eyes of the great bald eagle nesting each year in the dead black gum by the spring. Lack of teeth probably accounted for the turned-up, pointed chin and made the nose seem longer, so that, in profile, nose and chin almost met and made the face reminiscent of witches on broom-sticks in illustrated editions of the Grimms' *Fairy Tales.* The brow above the piercing eyes was boldly modeled.

"What color was your hair before it turned, granny?"

"Black—black as yer own." She put her hand up to her scant white hair, through which the scalp showed pink and shiny as a baby's. "My fust mister, he uster say hit be like a crow's wing, shinin' an' all. 'Spect had oughter stamp outen a leetle onion juice an' rub hit on these ere pesky bare spots—iffen so be hit's a day full o' sun, come morrow."

"Onion juice on your hair?" The Plant Woman sat up in amazement. "What in the world for?"

The Snake Woman sniffed disapprovingly. " 'Pears like ye be mighty triflin'. How come yer maw ain't nuvver larned ye sich as be of use? Ary fowkses knows as how onion juice, rubbed in servigerously, sprouts hair like weeds after a rain, iffen so be ye stand in the sun."

After this severe rebuke it seemed best to change the subject. "I wish I had my water-color paints here; I'd love to make a sketch of you and King, with the pink crape myrtle bush in the background."

"Whut be a sketch?"

"A painting, showing just how you look in colors —same as the pictures in the books Cella has at home. Wouldn't you like that?" The Plant Woman wanted a picture of the old woman very much, but she had flatly refused to be taken with the camera.

"I dunno. Hain't got no manner o' longin' fer sich like. Howsomever, I'm right peart when I'm smarted up, in my store dress an' all. Course, my workin' things hain't so much." She looked down disparagingly at the shapeless cotton dress she wore. Though clean and pressed, one could not mistake the fact that it was made of flour sacking; even after numerous washings the faded blue letters "ry's Best" showed across the front of the waist. Granny's skinny old arms stretched beneath the short flowing sleeves. The full gathered skirt came only halfway between knee and ankle—"so be I kin heft my feet."

This was the month of the Indian Thunder Moon, July, when heat waves dance across the young tobacco. A young moon hung, hot and burnished, over the swampland. The Snake Woman peered at it over her left shoulder, for luck. Yes, there was rain, so badly needed, in the downward sweep of its curved horns. She rocked on slowly in the creaking swing; her veined old hands slid gently down the velvety loops of the big snake on her lap.

"How long have you had King?" the Plant Woman asked.

"I disremember. Afore my second mister passed away he found him in the powsture by the north hammock. I heerd tell his kind is death to rattlers, so I made me a penetrate of milk, honey, an' molasses, an' brung him up by hand."

The rattlesnake skins drying on the fence? Yes, some of them were relics of his prowess; but he had to be watched right smart, else he et 'em with no regard for their value.

"I suppose he keeps your place free of all sorts of snakes, the harmless ones as well as those that are poisonous?"

"Yes, indeedy." Her voice was proud. "Hain't no snake dast show hisself roun' about. King even fights snakeses bigger'n he-uns. Iffen they beint rattlers, I 'lows him to eat 'em. He be partial like to cottonmouths."

The Plant Woman reached for her sweater and fastened it around her shoulders; a thin white mist was rising from the prairies. "Yes, I know. I saw a king snake the other day in the piney woods that had just swallowed a cottonmouth much larger than itself. The end of the snake's tail was still hanging out of the king's mouth."

"Why be King don' die from all these pizen snakeses? Seen lotsa ole rattlers bite him an' bite him. Nuvver bothers him a-tall."

"Because the king snake can't be poisoned by the bite of any venomous snake in the Americas. I don't know just why that is true, but it is a fact, nevertheless. Do you have many of the little coral snakes around here?"

"Sure. Hand me my snuff an' stick. Thanky kindly." She pushed the snuff stick firmly into her mouth. "Lessee now. I dig up two of 'em yisterday, in the corn lot. Wust is, thar be two of 'em with bright-colored bands aroun' 'em. They looks jest alike. One is pizen, an' t'other hain't. Don' know which to kill."

"There's a funny old rhyme that explains how to tell them apart—by the way the stripes join. The yellow bands on the poisonous snake always border the black stripes. The verse goes like this:

> Red and yellow, kill a fellow
> Red and black, nice to Jack.

If you remember that, you won't be in any danger. The coral snake, the bad one, is very poisonous, though; it belongs to the cobra family and is the only one of that family in America. It is more deadly than any of the other poisonous snakes, though it is so small—three feet would be a very large one. It doesn't seem to care to get around so much—not like the rattlers—it lives in the ground, or beneath the bark on trees, so that people are seldom bitten. It bites, and chews its poison into the wound, like all the cobras, instead of striking like the rattlesnakes and cottonmouths."

"What for be there two snakes lookin' jest alike?"

The Plant Woman wished she knew that herself. The disgusted Snake Woman opined it was just plain onery of Nature to play such a low-down trick on fowkses. She got up to put the sleeping King in his basket, which always stood near the foot of her bed, then came back to the swing. They sat awhile in silence. The night seemed soft, pulsing, and alive. Myriad swarming insects burdened the air with their cries, while the frogs and the owls added to the din. In the bay a wildcat yowled, singing a dirge to the new moon. Granny hummed softly to herself, part of an old ballad of which the Plant Woman caught only the following:

> What et ye for supper, Lord Randall, my son?
> What et ye for supper, my best lovèd one?
> What et ye for supper? Mother, spread my bed soon
> For I'm sick at the heart, an' I wish to lie doon.

"Bin hopin' Freeman and the boys ud come over tonight, an' bring a diamondback for a fight, hit bein' moonin' an' all." Her voice was eager. "I hope they come; I'd sure like fer ye to see one, bein' from the city an' all, an' a-missin' most everythin' in life! Iffen all the things ye tell about yer ignorance be true, I'd like mighty well to holp ye."

"If they don't come tonight, isn't there some way I can see King fight?"

"Oh, sure for sartin. I'll git word to ye, nuvver fear. The boys is sartin to come soon. They most alus has a snake or two, an' I heerd as how they ketched a mis' an' a mister on Bugaboo last night. Hides an' taller don' bring so much lately, so there's not so many hunt diamondbacks any more. 'Pears as if fowkses got their rheumatis most cured."

"You sell the skins and the oil, also?"

"Course. I make a right smart bit now an' agin. Taller fries out real quick like; an' 't ain't hard as hoein' taters. 'Sides, the meat's turrible good eatin'. My fust mister, he were mighty fond of hit."

"You mean you eat rattlesnake meat?" the Plant Woman cried in horror.

"Sure! Tastes jest like a spring fryer. I'll be jest proud to do ye some, come morrow." She dipped deep in the snuffbox, then sucked contentedly, with loud noises. Her guest said nothing for a while, then ventured a personal question.

"Granny, aren't you ever lonely, living here all by yourself?"

" 'Pears like I hain't bin near so lonesome since I had King." Her voice was tender. "I bin hopin' he'd kotch hisself a wife; but thar, seems like he's sot in his ways, like all men."

The woman stifled a laugh. "So you think men are set in their ways? And yet you were married twice?"

"Had bad luck, both times, 'pears like. The boy's pappy was a good man, but pulin'; an' they was tooken jest like him. All passed to lee'ard afore manhood with ummage [hemorrhage] of the stomach, but Jed. My second mister, he was took with the water disease, an' swelled until he nigh bust. I brayed him a powder of elderberries an' strawberry leaves, but 't was the Lord's will an' he passed away."

"Jed must have been a great deal of company for you, after losing all your other children. I'm so sorry that he could not have stayed with you."

"Plant Woman, he went agin the teachin' of the

Good Book. To the outland he went, a-lumberin' an' a-cuttin' high pranks with loose womern. They found him dead in a big swale whar a rattler bit him."

The Plant Woman shuddered at the thought of the man dying, in convulsions, all alone in the swamp. "How horrible," she cried. "The swamp country is so beautiful, but so cruel."

The Snake Woman leaned over the edge of the porch and spat accurately at a small lizard scurrying beneath a stone. "Yes'm, it sure be." She wiped the back of her hand across her mouth. "An' the cure be right by his hand. Thar be the rattlesnake master [rattlesnake plantain], an' all he need to do was to chaw the leaves. Hain't hit turrible?"

"You know a great deal about curing sick people, don't you? Freeman told me you used to bring all the children into the world, here in the swamp country. Don't you do that any more?"

"Well, 't is so. But, come late years, they mos' alus brings in a new uppity man from the outland, an' he disencouraged that I best care for womern after the baby is found, stead of afore, like alus. Course, I do so now an' agin, when I keers to. I found my ten all alone, with the holp of the mister."

"Tell me some of the medicines you use to cure sick people. I'm from the outland, so you need not mind telling them to me."

The old woman shrilled her loud cackle. "What's it wuth to ye?"

"What do you want? I'd like very much to learn some of your remedies."

She swung for a while in silence, thinking it over. "Do ye want to know how to keep the mister, an' how to git a husband, an' all sich?"

"Yes, indeed. Then, in case mine tries to get away, I'll know just what to do."

"Can I hev the smellin' water ye got in yer sack, an' the red stuff ye put on yer mouth?"

"Why, yes, granny! But wouldn't you rather have some money to buy something with—some nice white flour, or something like that?"

"No. 'Spect I'll look right peart when I git smarted up with the smellin' water an' the red paint. Mebbe I'll git me 'nother mister, I dunno."

Her guest went into the cabin and brought out a bottle of lavender toilet water, and a new lipstick of a flaming red. The old woman seized them quickly with her skinny hands. She sniffed eagerly at the perfume and twirled the lipstick to make it appear and disappear into the shield. After a little prompting she opined that the following prescriptions were sartin cures and the charms never failed.

REMEDIES:
Powdered snakeroot for headaches and coughs.
Ground persimmon sprouts for poulticing sores.
Juice of boxwood to cure toothache.
Puffball fungus to cure nosebleed.
Plantain leaves, crushed, for burns and bruises.
Corn meal and honey for sties on the eyes.
Tea of stem and fruit of Virginia creeper as a purgative.
Ginger tea for loosening of the belly (indigestion?).
Strawberries for fainting spirits.

Live frog cut in two and applied hot, a sure cure for
warts.

For giddiness or fever: Seeds of parsley, dill and rue,
Seeds of cellandine and fever-
few
Take equal parts of all these
worts
An' you'll be ready for any
sport.

Tea brewed of wild oranges and basil for yellow skin
(jaundice).

LOVE POTIONS AND CHARMS:

White moss from the skull of a murdered man, picked
in the graveyard at the full of the moon. Wear this
tied in a piece of blue cotton cloth around your
neck. Guaranteed to win any man.

Three drops of blood from a snake while it is still alive
(a snake is not supposed to die until sundown, re-
gardless of when it is killed). Mix this with a small
pinch of spider dust (ground spider) and stir well
into half a cup of "green corn." Guaranteed to kill
any rival who innocently drinks it and to bring
back the beloved one.

A lodestone from a deer (a hard substance sometimes
found in a deer) and carried in the pocket or
around the neck gives the power to produce twins
at will.

An eagle stone (taken from the bird while alive)
worn around the neck will keep husband or wife
faithful. If they stray burn seven—the mystic
number—sprouts of a young persimmon tree in the
fire, and the unfaithful one will have seven severe
pains and return home.

Take seven hairs from a black cat, seven scales from a

rattlesnake, and seven bits of feathers from an owl. To these add a hair from the head of the person you desire and a bit of nail paring. Cook these for seven minutes over a hot fire in the first rain water caught in April. Sprinkle the mixture on the clothes of the person to be charmed. Cannot fail.

SUPERSTITIONS:

If you drop a knife or fork, someone is coming.

Crushed rosemary herb in scuppernong wine inspires powers of the mind.

Sassafras root carried in pocket is a charm against all disease.

Snake eggs are a sure cure for stutters.

Anything dreamed while a piece of wedding cake is under the pillow will come true.

To insure fertility of your wife (or cattle), throw cow peas into a traveled road, so that they will be ground into the soil.

A stone with a hole in it hung over the bed of a pregnant woman assists the birth.

The fruit of the horse chestnut, carried in the pocket, will prevent any infectious disease.

If the whippoorwill cries near the house, someone in the family will die within a week.

The calling of a tree frog means rain.

The first one of a newly married couple to step over the doorsill will die first.

If a black cat licks her fur the wrong way it will either rain or trouble will come to the family.

Turn your pockets wrong side out to prevent sickness or death, following the hoot of an owl.

Sore mouth (thrush) in a baby can be cured by giving him tansy tea.

Never sweep under the bed of a sick person with a new broom; he will surely die or have fits (convulsions).

Wood that has been struck by lightning is unlucky. To remove the spell sprinkle it with greasy dishwater.

If you look in a spring at midnight on Halloween you will see, by the light of your fatwood torch, the face of your future husband reflected there.

"Heerd 'nough?" the Snake Woman asked. "'T ain't half what I knows. Could yarn ye about cures an' charms all night. But I hain't. I'm a-goin' to my bed an' git my beauty sleep."

CHAPTER SIX

King of Death

Two weeks passed before the fight came off between King and a giant rattlesnake caught by Obadiah on Bugaboo Island. Then, late one afternoon, Diah and a dozen or more men arrived with a stout box. They cooked their supper in the clearing and sat about talking and laughing in high good humor. All of them placed wagers on the diamondback's staying powers—everyone knew it had not the slightest chance of winning.

"He's got twenty-one rattles," Diah told the Snake Woman.

At dark, Freeman came, bringing a boy named Tom, a dusky handsome lad, part Seminole, whom he had secured as a guide for the Plant Woman on some of her collecting trips. She planned to visit the coast marshes on a hunt for the great sea turtles that come to the island beaches at this season to lay their eggs.

The fulling moon rose above the black tips of the pines and the men gathered near the cabin, with the exception of Obadiah, who lurked in the bush with his gladiator still safely boxed. Snake Woman settled herself on a tall stump at the edge of the porch and swung her feet free of the ground. There was no sign of the King, as yet. Freeman went over to the far side of the clearing.

"Granny, maybe King won't come," the Plant Woman whispered, suddenly chilled with the excitement and the strangeness of the scene.

"Nuvver fear. King senses 'em whether he be a-sleepin', or a-takin' hisself a ramble in the powsture. He'll be along."

Freeman squeaked sharply, imitating the metallic cry of a field mouse. So stealthily that only Tom's sharply drawn breath gave the Plant Woman warning of its approach, the warrior-guest appeared. Shaken from the box, in which it had raged helplessly, the rattlesnake came into the open, hungry, and ugly in disposition as only the lord of death can be. It paid no attention to the group of onlookers, knowing well, perhaps, its own deadly powers and the menace of its appearance. The Plant Woman drew back, in panic. Moonlight lay bright on the clearing and she could see the wicked eyes in the broad triangular head, their vertical jade line distended, and the olive-green plated back, ornamented from neck to tail in brownish black diamonds, with borders of pale yellow. Freeman imitated the squeaking mouse again. The snake's powerful body, nearly a foot in circumference and seven feet long, crawled swiftly toward the sound, leaving a straight, deep track. Even against the moonlit sand, the deceptive coloring, which masks these reptiles so dangerously well in the brush by day, suggested wind-blown patches of withered marsh grass.

Freeman stepped away in a hurry from his unsafe post, as decoy. A twig snapped sharply under his foot. Instantly the snake coiled and a staccato whir, sharp as a bell, trilled in the silence. The twenty-one rattles, thrust straight up toward the menacing head, centered above the beautifully decorated body, moved so rapidly that they were only a blur in the moonlight. Holding his pose arrogantly, the stranger faced the danger he sensed but could not see. Seconds passed. The warning notes dwindled to a faint buzz, and ceased.

But the sound had penetrated to the deep shadow in the unlighted cabin where the royal basket stood at the Snake Woman's bedside: or, if not the sound, some reptilian sense of challenge and a kill to be made woke the sleeper. One moment the open kitchen and the doorsill were only empty blackness; then it seemed as if the illusory edge of nothingness quivered.

A slim body, like a rope paying out, flowed from the darkness and through the moon rays on the porch with a speed that no rattlesnake could ever equal. The King had come! Fearless and immune, he darted straight at the intruder in his garden.

Rattles whirring, the diamondback swelled upward in his rage, as if powerful springs propelled his vibrating coils. Quick as light, he struck, sinking his two curved hollow fangs deep into the long thin black body, already rippling about his own. Again and again he struck. But like a smooth steel tape the black fighter whipped his slender coils round the threshing olive-green body, closer, and higher to the throat. Desperate, the diamondback tried to blind his foe, thrusting at the small oval head—like a second one, now, branching from his own neck. But King's head, which usually faced him, never came within reach of the fangs. Sometimes, in his fury, King turned and bit the rattler in the back of the head, though his teeth could do no harm. The snakes rolled over and over, in a tangled, writhing mass, from side to side of the clearing. The heavier body began to lose momentum; but the resiliency of the other was not lessened: it wound tighter and tighter. Presently the rattler's mouth gaped as if for air. Then the head no longer lunged, striking; it seemed to move not of itself, but only because of that constricting steel tape about the neck. The battle was over. The big diamondback lay limp and lifeless within the black coils. King relaxed his hold, quickly unwound himself from the dead body, and crawled away. Snake Woman gathered him up in her arms.

"The hide's yern, but ye leave the meat fer me to try out the oil for more rheumatiz cure," she said to Obadiah.

"How come King let him drop an' didn't start to et him?" Tom asked.

"Hee! Hee!" she cackled. "I brayed King nigh a double potion of warm milk for his supper. So as how he wouldn't be hongry for rattler meat." She carried him indoors to his basket.

The Plant Woman sank down on the porch, feeling a little weak. Next day she and Tom headed for the coast.

Wide sea marshes stretch for miles along the islands of the Georgia coast. They are cut by winding salt creeks and are broken here and there by little hammocks of cedar and scrub pine.

Since late afternoon Tom and the Plant Woman had paddled down a deep, tidal creek which, after meandering for miles through the reedy marsh, would bring them to the sea. Sometimes they pushed the boat into the reeds of the marsh, or pulled it high on a spit of sand, and watched, fascinated, the strange and beautiful things that glided past. The boy told the Plant Woman about the alligators that occasionally leave the big swamp to the west and cruise downstream with the ebb tide. This was rare, he explained, for gators seldom venture into salt-water creeks or rivers. Huge porpoises, six or eight feet long, swim in with the flood tide to feed on the shrimp and mullet and other small fish that abound in the marsh creeks. But the woman had seen neither of these rare sights.

Disappointed, she stood up in the boat and gazed across the grassy level to where the surf broke upon the ocean beach. The western sky was all flame red and amber; shoals of tiny oyster-white clouds drifted across the afterglow.

As she watched, a flock of skimmers flew low over the reeds, uttering their trumpetlike yaup-yaups. Their white and jet plumage was conspicuous against the water where they settled to feed. They opened their great red and black bills wide, the lower knife-like mandible plowing the creek for fish or other aquatic inhabitants. With a loud whosh-whosh of wings, a large flock of wood ibis swept slowly by and came to rest a little way from the punt. The boy had bent the tall grass over the boat, so that its occupants were hidden from view. Making a great clatter with their powerful, curved bills, the ibis gathered frogs and insects from the water, and dozens of small fish which rose to the surface to breathe.

The Plant Woman had never seen those birds so near before, and she watched intently. Tom touched her hand. "Flintheads," he breathed. She nodded, recognizing the aptness of the name when the big birds strutted past with the last of the evening light falling full on their bare, featherless heads. She noted Tom eying the gun longingly. She kept her hand on it.

Then—she caught her breath with wonder!

A bird with exquisite pink plumage slowly edged out from the center of the flock until it fed alone in the shallows. Its long bill, broad and flat at the tip, swung from side to side, like a mower's scythe swinging through meadow grass, as it skimmed small fish from the creek. Frequently both head and neck were submerged for brief periods. The beautiful bird was one of the few roseate spoonbills left in this country. From hundreds of thousands formerly inhabiting the Gulf states, the spoonbills have dwindled to a pitiful few hundred in Florida, Louisiana, and Texas, with an occasional stray found in other southern states. Feather hunters have killed them by the thousands to sell the gorgeous pink plumes to curio dealers for the tourist trade; and pot hunters, Indians and whites alike, have shot them for food.

Darkness deepened over the marsh. The ibis flock soared high into the air. Around and around they sailed, effortlessly, and then descended in wide white spirals to their roost in a hammock. The lone spoonbill went with them, his plumes trailing rose across the deep blue of the eastern sky.

Tom paddled swiftly down the creek, and the Plant Woman slapped viciously at the mosquitoes that swarmed about her head. As they neared the shore they saw that the tide was very high. The beach was little more than a narrow strip of sand; on one side the heavy surf broke in hissing phosphorescent foam, while on the other stretched the quiet waters of the marsh. They pulled the boat high up on the sand, anchored it firmly, and settled down to watch the big loggerhead turtles haul in on the rising tide.

Suddenly, from near by, above the monotonous pound of the surf came a long-drawn, tremulous sigh, deep and melancholy. The woman's eyes followed the boy's pointing finger. A hideous monster was dragging its vast bulk up the gently sloping shore, sighing as it came. The turtle crawled very slowly. Her body left a broad smooth furrow in the sand, with a ridge on either side made by her flippers as they pulled her three hundred pounds, or more, of weight along. In the water the heavy body has support and the turtle cleaves her way freely through the sea, her powerful flippers thrashing like propellers. But peril of death besets the female loggerhead from the moment she is forced ashore by the necessity of egg-laying. It is only with great difficulty that she breathes on land, because her weight presses her flat against the sand and prevents the normal action— somewhat like the alternate loosening and tightening of elastic—that stretches the plates of her underbody armor and brings them together again. She has to raise herself slightly on her flippers, a hard task in itself, take a breath, sink down again, and crawl on for a short space and keep repeating the process, or perish of suffocation. Many a loggerhead dies on the sand as she tries to make her way back to the sea after depositing her eggs. Loggerheads apparently have no sense of direction on land. If they get turned away from the sea, during the egg-laying, they crawl on into the marshes and die. Only female loggerheads are ever seen by man; the males never come to shore. The laying of eggs ashore seems to be the only instinct or need relating the sea turtles now to their primordial ancestors, which were land animals.

All during the hot nights of summer the female

turtles brave these dangers and crawl above ordinary
high-water marks on sandy beaches, where they ex-
cavate their nests in the warm sand. The young hatch
in August and September, at night, and make straight
for the sea, allowing no obstacle to force them to
crawl in another direction.

At last the big female reached a suitable spot.
She rested a short while, and then scooped out a round
pit in the sand with her hind flippers. The Plant

Woman watched closely, for she had been told that
the eggs are covered with sand thrown upon the
turtle's back during the process of excavation. The
eggs, she knew, would be laid one at a time, every
two or three seconds. Egg-laying finished, the loggerhead covered the nest carefully with excavated soil,
and not at all in the manner that the swamp folk had
described. "Diff'rent kinds of turtles," Tom insisted
later, in explanation.

Even before the turtle had reached the sea, the
boy was scraping the sand from the spherical eggs,
about an inch and a half in diameter, with a tough,
flexible shell. He gloated over the large number—
one hundred and sixty—refusing to leave any of them
to hatch. He started off along the beach looking for
other turtle "crawls." Within an hour he found two

more nests, which netted him a total of two hundred and seventy more eggs. A few were broken when he probed through the soft sand with a stick to discover their whereabouts.

"Don't take them all," the Plant Woman pleaded. "If everybody robs the nests that way, shortly there won't be any more turtles for anyone."

"Alus has bin, alus will be." He stalked off ahead down the beach to the boat with another load of eggs carried carefully in his hat. It was hopeless to argue. In some localities wild hogs make inroads on the turtle nests each summer; but this destructiveness is nothing compared with man's. Once the native hunter has found them, all the eggs are taken. None are ever left to hatch.

In silence they started on their homeward way up the water road, Tom making the proper turns unerringly, guided by signs invisible to his companion. Soon they were beyond the cry of the surf, but the Plant Woman sat still with her face turned seaward to the cloudless horizon of the starlit ocean. There, invisible to her, a giant turtle headed out to sea, cleaving her way swiftly through the great green swells.

CHAPTER SEVEN

Sugar in the Gourd

CELLA was awakened early by the throaty cries of two great horned owls that lived in a hollow tree on the edge of the swamp. Often, on moonlit nights, she had watched a dark shape plane swiftly, soundlessly down upon an unsuspecting marsh rabbit. There would be a squeal, a flutter of broad wings, and then, as silently as it had come, the big owl would float upward, a limp brown form dangling in its claws.

She rose, and then called and shook her young sister, Mar'lee. Sleepy sounds and stirrings were already coming from the other rooms. Soon after sunrise neighbor men would come to help with the log raising for the new addition house. As swamp folk go, Freeman's family were prosperous; it was no longer necessary for them to live a-cluttered in a three-room cabin. Two more large rooms, joined to the main dwelling by a covered "dogtrot," would give them the best house in all the swamp country.

Cella padded softly over to the huge chimney where heavy logs of charred wood rested on strong blackened andirons in the deep fireplace, and stirred up the embers until the fire blazed brightly. She lifted a pot from the clean white sand of the hearth, filled it with water for the coffee, and hung it on the pothook that reached out from the chimney's back, then ladled two spoons of fresh coffee on the old grounds in the coffeepot. What fun they would have at the raisin', she thought, while she sliced bacon for frying and stirred the grits into the thick, smooth mush of which her father was so fond.

Manthy came from the bedroom. "Cella, put the griddle on. Yer pappy'll have need of a mess o' hoecakes to stay him." She pulled the bacon farther from the flames.

Cella's eyes followed her mother, busy now running a greased rag around the smoking hot griddle. The griddle was the pride of her mother's heart— so much nicer to use for baking hoecakes than ashes. Manthy was a tall woman, still comely, soft voiced and deep breasted, who took life comfortably as it came. Her face was full of content, with little quirky lines of laughter around her eyes and mouth. "Her hair looks blue," Cella thought in amazement, as the firelight glinted on the thick white locks drawn smoothly into a knot at the back of her head.

"Goin' fer long sweetnin', maw." She crossed the kitchen, lifted the empty honeypot from its shelf near the door, and sped down a little path to the thatched springhouse, where wild honey was stored in piggins standing around the stone curbing of the spring. It was dark inside, so she propped the door open with a stone. The honey was cold and poured in thick golden gobs. A little splashed on the stones, and she leaned down and lapped it up with her red tongue, as greedy for sweets as a young possum for frost-kissed persimmons in the fall. One of her long yellow braids, not yet put up for the day, dangled in the water; she brushed it aside impatiently. From the house came the sound of her mother's voice, calling.

She picked up the heavy pot of honey, but paused and leaned against the smooth trunk of a big magnolia to see the dawn break in the east. One bare brown foot caressed the other as she gazed at the familiar scene. The old log house was gray with age—weathered and worn—and moss grew in little patches on its sharply sloping roof. Trumpet creepers twined about the great stone chimney and dropped long sprays of brilliant red and yellow blossoms toward the earth. At the back the split-rail fence, smothered in muscadine and jessamine vines, zigzagged around the cleared lot where Freeman and Obadiah milked the cows. Their voices drifted faintly to her on the breeze. Soon, now, they would carry the cans, filled with rich foamy milk, to the spring-house and set them in the water to cool. The light crept slowly up the sky, leaving the backdrop of the swamp the color of the sweet wild orchids that in spring laid a shell-pink coverlet over the bog lot. Okefenokee was a still black mass, but hundreds of young pines were etched sharply against the green fields of young cotton and tobacco, while row upon row of rustling, waving corn stretched down to the swale.

Manthy called again, impatiently, but the girl stopped yet another moment to gather an armful of brilliant blossoms for the old blue Wedgwood pitcher. Gre'-gre'-gran'paw brought it years and years ago from a fureen place—England, he called it. Cella studied on it as she followed along the crape myrtle hedge to the house. Gre'-gre'-gran'paw was a tradi-tion in the family. Gran'paw, who was nigh unto ninety-nine and slept almost all day in the sun, some-times told her stories about the olden days. Once, he said, Gre'-gre'-gran'paw took him on a trip to the coast, down the St. Marys River, and he looked way out across the sea. If you sailed straight on, after months and months, you'd come right back to the Georgy coast, 'cause the earth was round, like a ball. One could hardly believe it, seeing how flat were the salt marshes and the piney woods. If he could only meet someone who had done it, he said, it would be easier to believe. But what Gre'-gre'-gran'paw said, 't was so—'t was so!

All Freeman's family could read and write a

little. Cella had more schooling than the rest and knew all the words in McGuffey's readers, which had belonged to Gran'paw's father and stood in a long row on the shelf above the fireplace. Last winter a hunter from the North sent a whole box of books with pictures—the *National Geographic Magazine*, it said on their backs—and winter nights by the fire she had spelled out stories about all kinds of foreign lands and folks. And she made up her mind, right then, that one of these days she was going outland.

"It gramies me," she told her father. "Hearken to all the wonders in the world as set forth in this here book. It tells as how there are pictures that move jest as though they was humans and alive. I've heerd tell as how they be in Waycross, even. An' railroads, an' airplanes, like done come down once in the swamp; an' everything. All winter long I pine for 'em."

2

The family hurried through breakfast; the girls tidied the cabin and moved the chairs out on the long porch, while Freeman and the boys dug two big pits in the yard. They placed iron gratings over them on which to roast slowly, through the day, wild shotes from the swamp and haunches of cherry-red venison. Obadiah, the hunter of the family, wanted to kill a bear for steak, but his father forbade this, angrily. "Hain't nothin' in yer head but wind," he told him; "lessen ye be keerful ye'll be jest like Titterin' Tom, an' we-uns'll hev to shut ye up in a franzy house. Nuvver nobody in my family kills ary b'ar

in out season, when the ha'rs all fall out an' the hide's
no good for rugs. Ye hain't got a lick o' sense, 'pears
like."

The two younger boys were ordered to burn
down hardwood in the pits for hot, slow-cooking
coals, and Manthy and Freeman moved out the long
pine table and put planks across wooden horses to
serve as another. Cella brought from the cypress chest
two thin, hand-woven covers, one in pink and one in
blue, which Gre'-gre'-gran'paw brought from England; she surveyed her handiwork proudly, when the
tables were covered and the Wedgwood pitcher was
set in the center.

There were raw rations in plenty—white flour
and coffee and short sweetnin' (sugar); there were
small buckets of lard, sausages in casings, piggins of
wild rice, and dishes of herbs and peppers for seasonings. Turtle for stewing soaked in salt water; wood
ducks hung up already cleaned for pot-roasting; and
dozens of fish were strung on spits for broiling. Yesterday Obadiah had gone hunting and brought back
sacks of partridges and wild turkeys from the piney
woods around the swamp. Manthy decided to fry
the partridges in deep fat and serve them with wild
rice, and to make tiny white-flour dumplings in a
rich gravy to eat with the roast turkeys. Mar'lee was
scrubbing potatoes to be roasted in the ashes. On one
end of the plank table were jars of preserved huckleberries, blackberries, spiced wild grapes, and pickled
cucumbers, green tomatoes, and even mustard pickles, sharp and biting, to whet the appetite.

Manthy surveyed the piles of food with pride.

Freeman was a good provider, an' a law-abidin' man. Some said 't was agin the law to kill dur outa season, an' the gov'ment punished ye for it. Didn't make no sense to her, she thought, though she'd nuvver go agin Freeman. God made critters to provide food for his fowkses, didn't he? How else could they live?

Freeman and Obadiah were already at work notching the logs so that they would fit tightly into each other; thus the walls would stand firm and true and keep out the heat in summer and the cold in winter. Now the clear, ringing yodels of the early comers floated in from the swamp landing; other signal calls sounded from the run off the Suwannee. The men came from all around, from Cowhouse, Floyd, Black Jack, Chesser, and Billys islands, from Mixon's Ferry, from Race Pond, and even from far-off Fargo. They brought their womenfolks and children with them.

The women wore clean cotton dresses in tones of blues and browns and pinks, with sunbonnets of white or in matching colors. They walked awkwardly, on feet unaccustomed to tight store shoes; their shoulders were stooped from heavy work and cotton picking. The older, settled couples came first, the younger ones straggled in later; nearly all the younger women carried babies in their arms, and older children dragged on their skirts.

All the women bustled around contentedly and happily, gossiping, scrubbing wash boilers, ladling in the food to cook, and setting the boilers over the fires. Some watched the slowly roasting meats and others set the coarse china on the tables. The men built the new addition house rapidly, lifting the heavy cured logs into place, each one fitting smooth and firm in the wall. Many of the new houses in the swamp country were built of pine or cypress shingles, but Freeman held no brief for such. "What's good 'nough for Pappy is good 'nough for me," he'd say proudly.

The builders stopped only for a bite at noon, and by early dark the last bit of wet clay was plastered on the big stone chimney and the new addition house was nearly finished. Freeman surveyed it with delight. It was solid and comfortable, and when finished off with a porch and vines trained on, nary man in the swamp would have so fine a place as he. Big fires lighted up the yard like day, and smudges kept the sand flies from the eating men. The women talked together of births and deaths and marryings; the young children slept peacefully in the old house and the others played at games around the fires.

As soon as the edge was taken off their appetite they fell to yarning. Some man would tell how, long ago, the Seminoles lived in the big swamp and raided and killed the early settlers. Gradually, under the influence of good hot food and green corn, their tongues were loosened and one story brought another —tales of runaway slaves who hid in Okefenokee, of deserters from the Civil War who made boat trips down the Suwannee to reach the Gulf and what they thought was safety. The women drank scuppernong wine, expanded cheerfully in the glow it produced, and sucked their snuff sticks, but did no more than laugh at and applaud the stories of their menfolk.

Women in the swamp play a silent part in men's company.

The evening wore on and the laughter and funny sayings and jokes seemed funnier than ever. Cella sat curled up on the sill of the new addition house and listened. Her father was yarning now and the group was still, listening attentively.

"Well, as I was sayin'," Freeman continued, "last week I had a job to do at the sawmill an' I thought I'd take a short cut through the piney woods. I tuk my old cypress club, jest in case I met a b'ar or a hant. I hadn't gone fur when, quick like, I felt somethin' strike the stick—so hard hit nigh knocked hit clean outen my hand. Well, I looked down, an' thar was the biggest ole buster of a rattlesnake ever I did see, with his fangs caught fast in the wood. I knocked him loose an' hit him a lick, then I hung him over a big gallberry bush. He was so long his head an' tail dragged for nigh on a yard on each side. On I went, keerless like, a-singin' an' a-whistlin', but soon I noticed that somethin' ailed my old club, it was so big and heavy like.

" 'Great catawampus!' says I, 'that snake was so powerful pizen hit's effected my club; hit's all swelled like.' An' 't was so! Come time I got to the mill, I war a-draggin' the biggest cypress log ever come outen the swamp, so I had it cut up for railroad ties an' sold 'em in Waycross. The man as bought 'em said they'd line near a mile o' track, an' he'd guarentee that I'd get a right smart heap of money. But I bin done outen my lawful rights an' I'm a-goin' to have the law on him. 'Cause this mornin' I got a

piece of writin' sayin' as how it come on an' rained
on the track; an' the pizen in the ties got so weak
they shrunk up, like. So they sold 'em for tooth-
picks, an' sent me a dime." Loud yells and guffaws
greeted this bit of wit, but Freeman sat with a grave
face. It's not fitten to laugh at your own humor.

A loud yodel from the landing announced strangers, and Freeman answered. Old Fiddler opened the
gate and came in. A tall, swaggering boy accompanied
him. Freeman rose to meet them.

"Howdy, mens. Come an' et."

"Thanky, thanky. We et. Howdy, ma'am, an'
you, Miss Cella. My, ye git sweeter every day. This
here is Pompano Joe, from the Gulf. He's a right
smart hand with a banjo, so I brung him for a little
jangle."

3

The puncheon floor of split, hewn logs not yet
being laid in the new house, the children were cleared
out of the big center room of the old one. "Light-
heartsomeness never comes amiss, after hard work,"
Freeman said as Old Fiddler scraped the top of a
tune. The fat-pine torches flared in the night wind.
One of the men unwrapped his homemade fiddle and
proudly called attention to the strings of fox gut instead of cat. Then Pompano Joe tuned up—plunk,
plunk, ting, ting. A few men started a song; others
shuffled uneasily, but none took the floor.

"Come on, fowkses—let's go," shouted Freeman.
"Choose yer pardners!"

Instantly the crowd began to pair, and four couples took their places. Old Fiddler and his helpers played on and on. Freeman bowed low, hand on heart, before Snake Woman of Cowhouse, who was fragrant with lavender and radiant with lipstick. The crowd shouted in good-natured laughter as he swung the agile old woman to the center of the room, her seventy-seven years forgotten. Freeman laughed with them and sang a verse of the song:

> Choose yer pardners, time's a-flyin',
> Take yer places on the floor;
> Don' ye hear that fiddle cryin',
> Snaky Woman, evermore?

The room was full of light and laughter and dust from the flying feet of the dancing couples, four to a square. The deep shouts of the men were pierced with the shrill cries of the women, who followed their partners briskly, in perfect time to the music. The fiddlers played furiously.

> S'lute yer pardners. Bow perlitely,
> That's the motion, through an' through.

The men stamped their feet in a complicated shuffle and Snake Woman kicked off her shoes, growing tight on her corns, without losing a beat of the music. Freeman yelled:

> Swing yer corners, hop up lightly,
> Hail Ameriky! Hallaloo!

The dancers flung themselves back and forth across the floor, sweat pouring down their faces, the

beat of their feet shaking the house to its foundations.
Partners swung the nearest right and left.

> Fust foot forward, keep her diggin',
> Now ye sashay back agin!
> Never mind yer ragged riggin'
> So ye kiver naked skin.

Faster and faster the men swung their partners,
until the girls' feet often swung clear of the floor.
Little squeals of excitement were met with loud bel-
lows of laughter.

> Swing or cheat! keep a-scootin'!

And the girls swung the men opposite them or turned
back to their partners.

> Cross right over, now all swing.
> Hold yer hands up highfalutin',
> Look permiskus—that's the thing.

The ladies skipped merrily, while the men on the
corners danced, hopped, and stamped, everyone ex-
pressing the way he felt, but all coming together on
the final beat that marked the time. Now all the
dancers sang together:

> Lawsy, Lawsy. Look at Sweeter.
> That gal swings a soople toe.
> Crack yer heels thar, Bud, an' meet her,
> Bow an' smile an' so-an'-so.

> Balance all! Don' be lazy,
> Fly aroun' an' sweat yer shirt.
> Stomp yer feet but don' go crazy
> 'Cause somebody might git hurt.

All sashay! Clar to gracious,
Nuvver seen the like afore.
Swampers sure can dance audacious,
Sway an' bow an' weep no more.

Promenade all! Thar comes Andy.
Seat yer pardners—git a rest.
Mens, ye-all will pass the candy
To the gal ye loves the best.

The set ended. The crowd went outdoors to cool
off and drink more of the green corn and scuppernong wine. Freeman started to fill the squares for the
next dance. Old Fiddler struck up "Cotton-Eyed
Joe," nodding to Pompano Joe from the Gulf to sing.
Pompano reached out an arm and grabbed Cella away
from her partner. And as he danced, he sang:

Cotton-Eyed Joe, with a tune for the South,
Everywhere I go, I hear his big mouth.
Promenade, oh, Promenade!
I'd a-bin married twenty years ago
If it hadn't a-bin for knock-kneed, Cotton-Eyed Joe.
Promenade, oh, Promenade!

The faces of the men were flushed and they
called jokes about each other across the room. Some
of them removed their coats. Their blue work shirts
and overalls blended into a colorful pattern with the
cotton prints of the women. Most of the women were
now dancing barefoot, scuffling their feet at the corners in a smooth rhythm of their own, while the
men cut elaborate pigeonwings and improvised new
steps.

Old Fiddler led the other musicians from one tune to another—"Turkey in the Straw," "Hunkie Dorie," and "Wild Goose Chase." Snake Woman, her snuff stick held at a rakish angle, skipped lively as a cricket from one man to another; and the men begged for her favors. Others of the older women leaned against the wall and watched, dancing a few steps or keeping time with their feet when the tune swung into some catchy strain.

Then the fiddler struck up a favorite with old and young and Pompano Joe cried out: "It's sweet as a mockin'-bird in courtin' time," and sang the ballad through, substituting Cella's name for that of the girl in the song:

> One morn young Robin he did go
> Down in the swampland for to mow.
> He scarce had gone twice round the sweel
> When a pesky sarpent bit him on the heel.
> Oh, tum titty, titty tum day!
> Oh, tum titty, titty tum day!
>
> He threw the knife upon the ground
> An' shut his eyes and looked all round.
> He grabbed the sarpent in his han'
> An' ran right back to Purcell-an'
> Oh, tum titty, titty tum day!
> Oh, tum titty, titty tum day!

While he sang the foolish ditty, he looked straight at Cella. She blushed and slid in back of the singers, for shame. All of them laughed heartily and sang the repeat lines and stamped out the measure right lustily.

Oh, Cella dear, please come and see
This pesky sarpent has bit me!
Oh, Robin dear, why did you go
Way down in the swampland for to mow?
Oh, tum titty, titty tum day!
Oh, tum titty, titty tum day!

Oh, Cella dear, I thought you knowed
'Tis Pappy's grass and must be mowed.
Now all you boys a warnin' take,
Never get bit by a rattlesnake.
Oh, tum titty, titty tum day!
Oh, tum titty, titty tum day!

After this Pompano Joe was a great favorite. All the girls looked at him longingly and begged him to sing again. He sprang into the center of the cleared floor and sang and cut capers like a courtin' gobbler, until all the crowd was weak with laughter. He dared the young men to dance him down and threw his heels around in the Hook and Line. At last he danced Short Dog to the tune of "Sugar in the Gourd."

Sugar in the gourd,
Gourd on the ground.
Way to git it out
Is to roll the gourd around.

And the crowd accepted him as one of them, shouting their approval.

All too soon the fiddles, muted, played the good-night song of the swampland:

Run along, John, or I'll tell yer pappy
The way ye've bin a-courtin'.

CHAPTER EIGHT

Quiltin' Kivers

THE mockingbirds were singing from every tree and bush in the lane leading to Freeman's house. There was a busy stir about the place: oxen and Negroes in the field, Freeman and Obadiah down on the riverbank repairing the landing, all the men singing as they worked. Open fires burned slowly outdoors under large kettles full of melon rind. Manthy was preserving. She went briskly from one vessel to another, stirring carefully with a large wooden spoon. On the long table beneath the live oak stood row upon row of six-quart pots of clay, rinsed clean and

waiting for the hot spiced peel. Snake Woman of
Cowhouse, wearing a clean blue dress, sat in the shade
slicing the crisp rind into a bright yellow bowl. She
paused occasionally to rebuke her amateur assistant:
"Plant Woman, did yer mammy nuvver larn ye
nothin'?" Sunlight filtered through the leaves and
made dappled shadows upon her white hair and flung
a golden aura round the immense sunflower heads
bowing on their tall stems behind her.

By ten o'clock the preserving was finished. The
iron pots were cleaned and taken indoors, and Cella
went briskly about filling them with good things for
the midday dinner. Black-haired, twelve-year-old
Mar'lee cut into small pieces the sweet meat of the
loggerhead turtle Pompano Joe had brought last night
from the coast. It had soaked in salt water since
break of day and now would be boiled with onions,
green peppers, and seasoning. Later, the delicate white
meat would be dipped in beaten egg, rolled in corn
meal, and fried in deep fat. A thick, tasty soup, with
diced carrots, tomatoes, okra, and small Irish potatoes
would be made from the broth. With the meat Manthy intended to serve piping hot white-flour biscuits,
fried green tomatoes, and potatoes baked in the ashes.
There was boughten green China tea for those who
wanted it. Freeman had traded three dozen eggs for
a whole pound at the little crossroads store only yesterday. But Manthy and many of the older women
who had been invited to the quilting preferred a
pungent drink brewed from the leaves of yaupon,
the swamp holly.

The first guests had arrived; the big room in the

new addition house buzzed with chatter as they laid their stiffly ironed sunbonnets carefully on the high bed and hunted out their scissors and thimbles from the deep pockets of their cotton and calico frocks. This was womernfowkses doin's. No men were allowed. The women gazed about them in awe and envy. Manthy was a master hand for smartin' up. Even the homemade furniture looked better than the store chairs they had saved for months to own. There were straight-backed pine chairs, made more than a generation ago, with legs stubbed from wear on the puncheon floor, and pieced cushions of cotton tied on the seats. The bed of sweet gum in the corner still cast off a faint fragrance from its hardened aromatic sap. Over the cords, which took the place of springs, was a double mattress of softened cornhusks and a feather bed of the finest and downiest goose feathers covered with soft cotton sheets and pieced quilts. The top spread, in gay reds, blues, and greens, was Cella's favorite pattern, the Double Wedding Ring. The cypress chest beneath the window held Cella's personal things, collected against the day when she would leave the homesite for a place of her own. A thick, black bearskin, scraped and cured by Obadiah, was flung carelessly across it; another lay before the fireplace. Rag rugs, braided into squares and oblongs, made bright splashes here and there.

The Snake Woman, padding in and out so lightly on her horny bare feet, stopped to finger the soft yellow curtains blowing at the glassless window. She crossed the dogtrot to the old house and spoke to Cella, who was busy with the dinner. "Purty color, yellow. Hit's been so long since I dyed ary piece I've plumb forgot the *de*rections. What's your maw bile to git that 'ere?"

The girl looked up with a start. "Yellow? Oh, the curtains? Maw soaked chips from the yellowwood tree that Gre'-gran'paw brung back from the outland. He was a master hand at rovin', an' alus brung back things to help out cheer in the house."

Manthy stood on a chair in the big room, hanging heavy cords from hooks to suspend the quilting frames at the proper height, so that the women could quilt while sitting down, two to a side and one on each end. The floor had been freshly swept, and two quilt linings of heavy dyed unbleached muslin were spread out, ready for the smooth layers of cotton that would serve as fillers. The Plant Woman looked admiringly at the bright colors, wondering how they were obtained. Bought dyes, she guessed, and asked a question.

"No, ma'am," Manthy answered emphatically. "We-uns uses only things from hereabouts. This green," pointing to the glowing jade-green lining on the floor, "hit's a purty color, hain't hit? I biled the muslin in a brew made from indigo plants an' a few pieces of bark from red maples. I set the shade with lye from wood ashes. After the goods dried I dipped hit agin in yellow dye made from biled leaves and bark of sweet leaf, as grows round the cypress ponds. Blue and yellow alus makes green," she explained kindly.

"And this gorgeous red?" fingering the brilliant crimson lining for the second quilt.

"Sure is purty. Made from pokeberries, but hit

hain't fast dye, Plant Woman. Runs like in washin'. But these be Cella's quilts, an' she's partial like to bright colors. The other linin's be purty, too. I used bark of sassafras for orange, an' buckthorn an' shoe-make for diff'rent kinds of yellow, an' red root for pinkish brown, an' queen's-delight—that's a medicine, too, for worms in the blood [spring fever]—for black."

Two patchwork covers were spread wide and placed over the cotton-covered lining on the floor, edge to edge, and basted into place. The Plant Woman went down on her knees to examine them and exclaimed with delight. Hundreds of little pieces were sewed together with fine stitches to form a pattern. The top for the green lining was the Snake Fence pattern, in shades of yellow and pinkish brown; the other cover was Joseph's Coat, and certainly every type of color and patch was represented. Before her dazzled eyes were spread dozens of others, to be quilted up during the long winter nights. The names were enchanting: Wild Goose Chase, Lover's Knot, Buzzard's Roost, Star of the East, Log Cabin, Strangers, Bird of Paradise, Cherokee Rose, Odds and Ends, Patience, Widows' Troubles, Forbidden Fruit, Hen and Chicken—and each was different from any of the rest.

The side frames were laid beside each quilt, then the end pieces were bound on with stout cord and the quilts stretched into shape, with the ends firmly fastened. As soon as the quilts swung from the cords, the women pulled up their chairs and started to sew, six to a quilt, using fine, even stitches through the top, cotton, and lining, and following the agreed pattern. Not only must every quilt top be worked out in an individual pattern, but the stitching to finish it must also follow a fixed design.

Guests who were not working stood around and joked and laughed and teased each other. Their turn would come after dinner, as four quilts must be finished that day. Mar'lee swept the dogtrot clean, brushing in front of Cella, just coming in the door, her arms filled with wild flowers to decorate the table: rose-pink and pure white sea stars, pale blue lobelias from the marsh, and late-blooming lilac passion flowers from the sandy spots in the woods.

"Hee! Hee!" Snake Woman cackled loudly through her scarlet lips and shoved her snuff stick into the corner of her mouth. "Sweep in front of ye sure sign ye'll nuvver be married! Hain't no use ye makin' sheep's eyes at Pompano Joe." Squeals of mirth greeted this sally; Cella blushed fiery red and ran from the room.

"Yes," Manthy acknowledged, " 'pears as how the young-uns are thinkin' of lovin' and marryin'. Belike come cane grindin', ye-all will have invites to Cella's pledge-troth to Pompano. Freeman's makin' palmity talk as how she be too young, but I hold with no sich. She be a womern grown, an' she can cook an' redd a house. Hain't as if Pompano was a mortworp—he's got a fine job in the gov'ment, holpin' out nursin' pines."

"Nursin' pines? What be sich?" Snake Woman wanted to know.

" 'Pears like the gov'ment is skeered the pine trees gonna give out, so they is a-growin' thousands an' thousands of baby pines. A nursery, they calls hit. An' they pay a passel of money to up-smartin' men who keer for the trees."

Work stopped. They looked at each other in amazement. Cash money for settin' out and nursin' trees? Why, there were millions of trees in the swamp and the piney woods. Was plumb foolish!

"What for the gov'ment need more trees? Hain't no use for all the trees thar be!" Freeman's maiden sister tossed her head angrily.

Manthy's soft drawl came soothingly. "Now, Sophrony, hain't ary need to be gramied. Pompano did say as how he 'lowed they needed extry trees for paper. Seems right foolish to con*tem*plate a-turnin' trees into paper, but that's men's business, an' I 'low we-all hain't no call to bother."

After dinner, work went smoothly and well. The talk was all of womern's doin's—of death, of sickness, of signs and portents, and of the everyday happenings of their lives. Sophrony told as how, only a few days gone, she'd had to pass the old bury'n ground at mornglowm, a-huntin' a sow an' little uns a-headin' to run wild in the swamp. Now, as everybody knows, only hants an' specters are abroad at that hour, an' she hurried an' hurried an' cast fearsome glances over her shoulder.

Just when she thought she was safely past, and paused to get breath into her body, a crashing sound, like thunder guns, held her rooted to the spot. And then with a rushing, roaring noise, a wind, stronger than ever blew before, lifted the bonnet from her head; and when she dared to look the graves had opened. And the dead awoke and poured forth, a spirit army on the move, a hundred thousand strong.

"Great caterwumpus!" Snake Woman leaned forward, staring. "Whut did ye do, Sophrony?"

Sophrony had dropped flat among the weeds and covered her eyes. Still she could see their leader, because he was a giant man, taller than the tallest cypress, and glowed like a lightning bug in the darkness; and lightning flashed from his tongue as he spoke, withering and burning all that it touched. The bones in his skeleton rattled so loud, people in near-by towns hastened to cover their crops from damage by hailstones; and the finger with which he pointed the way was large as a cypress log and dripped such rivers of blood that the fish in the creeks round about were drowned.

And then, when she was near dead of fright, the army reached the Suwannee and embarked in boats of fire. And they sailed—and they sailed—away into the silver mist, as silent as the sunlight.

" 'T is fitten ye should have ventures, Sophrony," Manthy allowed, genially. " 'Cause ye're a noticin' womern, for sartin. An' ye can tell all ye seen."

Presently Snake Woman turned to the outlander, politely.

"Plant Woman, iffen ye got a venture or a yarn to tell, we'd be pleased to hear it. I bin thinkin' as how ye're alus studyin' on plants an' trees. Mebbe ye know somethin' about the gov'ment nursin' trees, an' sich foolish. Be thar ary sinse to it?"

"Tell 'em what ye told me," said Manthy, "iffen so be ye're willin'."

The story of the pine nursery, interspersed with

innumerable questions, some of them keen and intelligent, others far from germane, went on for an hour or more, while practiced fingers kept busily at the quilting. This is the gist of the tale:

Within a few miles of Okefenokee there is an immense plantation of young pine trees, nursed by government employees. When the Plant Woman saw them, they looked like small green shadows on the white ground. In time these baby pines will be transplanted, to aid in the reforestation of the coastal plain. Rural schools in Georgia are now teaching the underlying principles of forestry to the farmers of the future, so that they will not destroy acres of timber by burning them over to make pasturage for their half-wild cattle. Pine pulpwood promises them as great a prosperity as ever cotton brought to the Old South.

Recently pine pulpwood has been used to make a tough wrapping paper known as kraft, the demand for which apparently is limitless. It takes at least twenty-five years, and generally longer, for newly planted spruce and fir to grow to a size suitable for pulpwood in the North. Southern slash pines grown from seed increase approximately one inch in diameter each year. But until Dr. Charles H. Herty found a simple, inexpensive way to use the quick-growing pines of the South, it was commonly believed that only the pitch-free conifers, such as fir, spruce, and hemlock, could be used for paper manufacture. Dr. Herty is a former President of the American Chemical Society. With the help of the Chemical Foundation and the State of Georgia he established and maintained a laboratory at Savannah, where he proved that the apparently impossible could be done.

Kraft paper mills are now being built in Georgia and Florida. In one mill alone the output is said to be approximately two hundred tons a day, with a market value of about $115 a ton.

Along the Gulf coast more than a half million acres of pineland have been bought for one mill alone. And a forgotten town named Port St. Joe will soon be re-established and as thriving a port as it was a hundred years ago.

"How come sich a town to be fergotten? What was all the fowkses in it doin'?" Snake Woman asked.

"There were no folks left. You see, a sailing ship brought yellow fever to Port St. Joe. Not enough men could be found to dig graves for those who died."

They were interested. They really wanted to know. But the Plant Woman could not flatter herself that they had thrilled to the prospect of a vast new industry as they had to Sophrony's personal experiences while hunting her little pigs in the graveyard.

CHAPTER NINE

The Phantom Deer of Carry's Sock

T HE day was bright and hot. A "hantle" of
men sprawled in comfort beneath the giant water
oaks on Carry's Sock Island. It was one of those days,
as Freeman said, "when ye'd bet yer last pinch of
backy that the fish would bite like all git out, but
they sartin sure hadn't lived up to expecterations."
The fish fry had been a failure; but the fish would
begin to do business again shortly—nobody worried.
He grinned as he thumbed tobacco into his old brier.

"Reckon ye need entertainment. What would ye like best to hear about, Pompano?"

The black-haired boy looked up, smiling. "I'd like hearin' about how this island got hits funny name."

"Hit's called Carry's Sock 'cause of the shape of the island, like a sock. Dunno who diskivered hit, mebbe a gal called Carry. But thar's a right smart funny yarn told about this island. Hit's hanted, that's what! An' by the ghost of a dur, too. An' all the fowkses nighabouts call it the fantoom dur of Carry's Sock. Ye hain't heered about hit? No? Well, 't was like this." Freeman pulled hard on his brier, then laid it carefully by his side and began.

"When the world was fust made, no fowkses lived in Okefenokee, only snakeses, alligators, birds, an' painters, all sich. But after a time the world got awful crowded an' the Injuns moved into the swamp, an' they built up big heaps of dirt to put their church-house and their cabins on. Hain't ye bin to Bugaboo Island, to see 'em? Thar's two big mounds over thar. Well, anyway, the Injuns was ruled by a womern and, strange to tell, they lived happy an' contented. Funny, hain't hit, how they could be contented, men bossed by a womern?

"Well, the swamp didn't look then jest like hit does now, but thar was moss hangin' on the trees jest the same. Hit's int'restin' about what made the moss. Gre'-gran'paw used to tell us about hit the way the Seminoles, who lived here when he came, told him. They said as how the North Wind and the South Wind had a upscuddle, an' the South Wind got licked to a frazzle. Course, that skeered everybody 'most to death 'cause, if the North Wind settled down in the swamp to live, everything would die of cold an' all the Injuns would starve to death. So everybody prayed an' sang songs; an' the big bosses of the sky got togither an' sent a rain like thar nuvver was afore. With the cold wind in here the rain froze on the trees in long icicles; an' then the sun come out blazin', hottern ever afore, an' dried the icicles into moss. Course the North Wind tried to blow hit away, but hit had no effect on the moss a-tall! That made the North Wind so durn mad hit went up north and stayed thar.

"Everything was fine for hunerts of years, till a evil speret come to live with the Injuns. She was young, an' purty as a bay tree in blossom; but she put a sure-'nough spell on 'em, an' they died like fish in droughttime when the cypress ponds dry up. Things got wuss an' wuss. Then, one night when the moon was fullin', the womern who ruled 'em had a dream. In this dream the gods told her if she would do like they said all the troubles an' sorrows of her fowkses would be ended. But they told her, too, that her own life on earth would be over. Now, that were purty hard, weren't hit? But she had grit an' she done hit!

"She kivered over a deep bog spot with leaves an' sich, so hit looked firm an' safe. Then she hid along the trail an' waited. Soon the evil speret come trippin' along, an' fell in the bog, whar she sank most out of sight. She had lotsa power, sich as shootin' lightnin' from her fingers, an' makin' snakeses come outen her mouth, but she couldn't git loose from the bog!

"Then the good womern said: 'Bring back all my people to life, an' I'll help ye outen the bog.' The evil speret didn't have ary choice a-tall. So she brought all the fowkses back to life. There was great salubriations in the Injun towns; but the young womern was very sad, 'cause on the next day she must give up her life in Okefenokee an' go to the gods as she'd promised. Warn't that awful?

"She left early next day, at mornglowm, an' traveled on an' on. Purty soon she come to the home of the Ingun gods. I disremember their names. 'Here I be,' she said. 'What be ye-uns a-goin' to do with me?' Well, the gods had no idee how purty she was till then—not seein' her close to—an' the biggest god decided to keep her for his wife. 'How would ye like to live in a cloud castle?' he said. 'Ye could have yer choice of colors—we got all the colors of the rainbow—if ye'll stay with me.' Well, she stayed for a little, an' then she pined an' pined for this swampland, where she'd lived happy for so long. He felt sorry about hit, but he couldn't think of ary way of turnin' her into a human agin. An' right thar an' then he had a smart idee. 'How would ye like to be a critter,' he asks her, 'an' go back to the swamp to live?' Well, she thought it would be bettern stayin' in a cloud castle; but for days an' days she couldn't make up her mind what kind of a critter she'd be. At last the god tuk matters in his own hands an' made her into a dur—just the handsomest dur ye ever did see. Pure white, she is, an' she lives here, on Carry's Sock.

"They do tell as how she is queen of all the dur; not weak and skeery like the common dur we know, but brave an' proud. Pappy, he's seed her often, when the bucks whistle in the fall. He says she can outrun any critter ever lived, that she's fastern the wind, and nuthin' can ever harm her 'cause the god made her *im*mortal—better than humans, that means. Not many swampers has seed her, but all know she's here, an' some has even tried to trap her. But noan'll ever git her, 'cause she can make herself *in*visible, if she wants. Mebbe she's croppin' close by ye this minute, Pompano."

A swift wary motion went through the group, heads turning, surreptitious glances darting under lowered lids to the lush green grass and the tree shadow where the Gulf boy lay. Pompano's black eyes were wide and glistening.

"Did ye ever see her, mister?" he asked, breathlessly.

"No, lad. I hain't nuvver seed her, myself. But I've heerd her often, callin' an' callin'."

CHAPTER TEN

Cane Grinding

SUMMER was over. It was cane-grinding time in the swamp country. Wild plum thickets showed gay crimson at the edges of the cane fields, where partridges whistled and larks rose and sang from the stubble. Young persimmon trees bent nearly to the ground under their heavy load, waiting for the first frost to mellow and sweeten their golden fruits.

Under the outdoor shed cane juice was bubbling and frothing in the big open kettle. Cella stirred the foaming syrup with a long-handled dipper to keep it from boiling over. The hot fire in the brick furnace cast flickering shadows on her pale blue dress and flaxen hair. Pompano Joe came and stood beside her as she worked.

All during the fall he had watched the various duties of the swamp farmers with interest. In his fisherman's world down on the Gulf he couldn't see cotton picked, potatoes banked, corn stored in a log crib, nor help to overhaul a cane mill—two big iron rollers set vertically on a heavy pine frame, with a crooked sapling cut and fitted in the proper place for a lever, the lower end almost touching the ground, and the upper swinging free as a balance. It was exciting to watch the ox, hitched to the end of the lever, start on his patient treadmill journey, while Silas fed the sugar cane to the slowly grinding rollers. A small trough in the mill frame caught the juice and led it to a barrel, covered with fine cheese-cloth to strain the impurities. "Pummy"—cane pulp —fell from the other side of the mill, and two large barrels were filled to the brim with the pale greenish liquid.

Cella dipped a little wooden paddle in the cane foam and handed it to Pompano for his first taste of the homemade syrup. Slowly the contents of the ket-tle changed in color to a warm amber. When it showed glints of golden red and tiny bubbles came bursting to the top, Cella called her father to draw the fire: the first pot was done. Some of the men came out with Freeman and helped him empty the steam-ing liquid into a long cypress trough to cool, then they filled the kettle for the next boiling.

There were voices and laughter in the brightly lighted house. Manthy appeared in the doorway, calling. Hand in hand, Cella and Pompano Joe went in where the neighbors, assembled for the betrothal feast, awaited them with the preacher from the outland, who had been invited to make the announcement and share in the fun. The big room was crowded. The guests, dressed in their best clothes, were all agog to hear when the wedding would take place. The preacher held up his hand for silence. And then he plighted the troth of the swamp girl, Purcella Amanda, to Pompano Joe Portygee, outlander, of Cedar Keys, way down on the Gulf in Ameriky. "I myself shall marry them come seven o'clock on Twelfth-night. All ye here assembled are invited to be present to witness." Then he kissed Cella and wished her joy; and all the guests brought forth their pledge gifts of handmade towels, dishes, bright lengths of cloth, and the richest man in the swampland added a shiny silver dollar.

After the betrothal supper, the games began. Dancing was not allowed, in deference to the preacher, but Stealin' Partners, Fancy Four, and Twistification were almost as good. All these romping games were played to music.

"Twistification," yelled Old Fiddler; and the lines began to form, the girls on one side and the boys on the other, with room for Pompano and Cella to march between them in dancing step.

> Oh, come along, my pretty miss,
> Oh, come along, my honey.
> Oh, come along, sweet sugar lump,
> An' we won't go home till Mon'y.

An' now I turn my sugar and tea,
An' now I turn my honey.
An' now I turn my sugar and tea,
An' now I turn my darlin'.

At the words "now I turn my sugar and tea," Pompano Joe swung Cella so hard that her feet cleared the floor, which brought loud laughter and applause. All quick-stepped in a promenade, then the lines formed again. This time they sang:

London Bridge is fallin' down,
Fallin' down, fallin' down,
Oh, girls, remember me!

London Bridge is fallin' down,
Fallin' down, fallin' down,
So, heigho! Ladies turn!

Pompano Joe whispered to Cella, "Whereby be this diff'rent from dancin'?" And she whispered back, in righteous indignation, "Course this hain't reg'lar dancin'! This be *Christian* dancin'!" He was still unconvinced, but silenced.

When the lull came in the play, the women took possession of Cella, and Pompano Joe slipped out of the hot room to see how the cane cooking was getting on. He found many of the men sitting in the warmth of the fire, telling tall tales of the swamp country. Corn liquor had passed around freely, and the crowd was jovial. Freeman was busy skimming the boiling syrup and putting it carefully to one side: cane beer, with a sweet-sour taste, would be made from the fermented skimmings and, later, would form excellent "buck" for a wildcat still.

The preacher sat on the big chopping block and

sipped a glass of the warm sweet cane juice. A bright shooting star sped across the sky and dropped behind the swamp. Gran'paw, whom all thought asleep in his padded rocker, piped up. "See that? Hain't that purty? But hit hain't near so nice as the night hunerts of stars fell on Okefenokee."

"What's that you said, gran'paw?" The preacher leaned forward and looked across at the old man. "I never heard anything about it."

"Hee! Hee!" cackled the old man. He thrust a piece of cane into the boiling syrup, scraped it around the edge of the pot, then blew on it to cool it a little before sticking it into his toothless mouth. "I heerd my pappy tell often as how, come November, shootin' stars kivered the land, thick as feathers on a wood duck's breast."

"Go ahead, mister," the crowd begged, good-naturedly. "Tell about hit."

Glad to be the center of attraction, the old man began in his quavering voice: "Well, Pappy 'lowed as how hit was fair late in the fall, an' he an' Mammy was a-settin' up till all hours, a-yawnin'. Mammy, she were the talkingest womern ever a man did see. Well, along afore midnight, thar come a whole flock of shootin' stars, an' the air was jest filled with flashes from 'em. Pappy was larned an' alus was one for re-memberin' times an' numbers. Hit were the year 1833, I heerd him tell hit often. He said the stars fell for hours and hours, with light flyin' out from 'em like lightnin' flashes; an' thar was floods of yellow light over the sky. All night long the stars fell, not hittin' the earth, but flyin' back an' forth an' dartin' here an' thar, till they ceased at last, come morn-glowm. An' all night long the fowkses went a-polin' their boats, or standin' on their porches, all the family togither, a-callin' the distress call through the swamp country—thinkin' the great day of judgment was come. Bein' so bright, as hit were, they nuvver seed so many hants in Okefenokee afore. Hants of b'ar an' dur an' gators, biggern ary critters livin' now, an' giants an' evil womern sperets, a-fleein' an' a-flyin' an' a-callin' the distress call, their voices not soundin' like they come outen fleshy throats, but thin an' shrill, like specters."

CHAPTER ELEVEN

Wild Is Wild

Cool nights had come and there was a snap in the early morning air as autumn moved on toward winter. Corn grinding done, Obadiah was free to indulge the born naturalist in him: to pole idly along the runs, usually with his own pup, Blockie, in the boat with him, and watch the wild life of land and water.

"I wouldn't dast take Scavenger or Brisket, 'cause they is hunters, an' thar's times when no man on earth can hold in huntin' dogs," he said to Pompano, as he moved his feet to make room for Blockie. "But Blockie'll lie still as a stone iffen I say the word. I never seed a dog, like this young un, to git a idee. 'Pears like he's most human." Then he added, "Only he hain't. He's a dog, plumb full of critter sense. His mammy got bit by a rattler an' I brung him up on a bottle. Ary cold night he jumps on my bed an' slithers down under the kivers."

"I cotton to that black hide, myself. An' his tan spots is purty. He's sleek, like a otter." Pompano ran his hand over Blockie's coat. The young dog paid no attention to him: his eyes were fixed on his master.

"Hopin' to see otter today," Diah said. He knew where there were otter slides and headed the boat in that direction. Pompano had not seen otter until he came into Okefenokee: "Git a sight of money for their pelts, I heerd tell."

Yes, Obadiah said; but he didn't enjoy killing critters so full of frolic, which had made him laugh heartily many a time. Some hunters went after them with dogs, specially trained—otterhounds, they called them. Diah thought it was a waste of good dogs, no matter how much money there was in otters' pelts. The otter was so lithe and swift and such a strong swimmer, he could dive under the slower hound, break his leg, or get him by the throat, and pull his head under water and drown him. Otters stayed under water and didn't need to come up to breathe for a much longer time than any other animal, "lessen hit's a fish." But otterhounds were fierce and smart, and two or three of them together usually killed the critter.

The run led past a sandy shore topped by trees, bare of leaf now, and persimmons, heavy with fruit. The island was a happy hunting ground for raccoons. These were, of course, the southern variety, yellowish instead of gray, with the same dark rings and dainty black gloves. They were out in numbers today, enjoying the sunshine and gathering food. Their fluffy tails were like little clouds among the branches of the pecans, as they darted about picking green nuts with their black fingers. Eager, small, furry faces, with that appealing naïve expression that Nature has given to this diminutive species of the bear family, peered out from among the boughs of a persimmon near the shore. One moment the tree seemed to be jerking in the sudden clutch of an erratic wind, with its red-gold balls tumbling to burst on the ground; then the vigorous shaking ceased and half a dozen raccoons, or twice that number, came racing down the trunk. Without jostling or other family rudeness, each raccoon deftly seized a persimmon for himself, sat erect holding it in his paws, and nipped delicately.

A small grass snake, intent only on its own objectives, unwisely crawled along the outskirts of the circle of persimmon eaters. There was a leap, the flirt of a plumy tail, a swift pounce: the grass snake's wanderings were ended forever by sharp teeth meeting through its neck.

"Snake meat with 'simmons. That's a mess of vittles, hain't hit? Keep a lookin' an' see him clean hit," Obadiah muttered. Pompano watched with glistening eyes.

The raccoon's native speed and grace were somewhat hampered by the dragging snake, which was about nine inches long, though hardly thicker than a pencil; but he came on resolutely to the water's edge.

"Gators must snap 'em up sometimes when they come to water," Pompano thought, and Diah said they did, "snapped down aplenty."

"Lawsy! he's washin' it!"

The raccoon was apparently oblivious of the perils lurking in the pool. He gave his whole mind to the important business in hand. Squatting solidly on the very brink, he closed his jaws more tightly on the snake's neck, clasped his paws firmly about its body, and sloshed it up and down in the water, much as a careful laundress does with a fine garment that will bear no rubbing. The skillful little paws moved, taking new grips here and there. An awkward job, washing this long body; and nine or ten inches of snake are quite a pull on one's jaw, too! But at last the flesh was cleansed and fit to eat, according to the pure-food regulations of raccoons, and the fastidious hunter began his meal.

"They alus wash their meats," Diah said, "but not alus their nuts an' fruit, leastways not as I seed. Glad no gator were hangin' round." Pompano nodded.

"Swamp fowkses sing a little rhyme about that branch crick runnin' back of the island. Likely a gator got somebody's sow thar once." Diah chanted:

Old sow sank in the deeps of the branch
While the raccoon fiddled an' the possum danced.

Pompano laughed and said he had not noticed any possums, he had been so absorbed in watching the raccoon wash its snake.

"Bound to be some," Diah answered. "Listen to this un:

> Possum hangin' in the tree,
> Raccoon on the ground;
> Raccoon say, ye stingy cuss,
> Shake them 'simmons down!

I could feel Blockie jest a-quiverin' to jump out an' frolic 'em back up the trees. But he lay quiet like I told him." He patted the dog's head.

Diah pushed the boat forward. After a time he turned into a fish creek. A short while ago he had seen otter up this creek, he said.

"Otters has notions like humans about stayin' out of other fowkses' powstures an' keepin' strangers

out of theirn. They'll go a-roamin' an', all at once,
they'll see a sign that tells 'em they've went past their
own land an' got in their neighbor's cornpatch. An'
they'll turn right around an' git out of thar, an' come
home a-runnin', or a-swimmin', like a hant were after
'em. Iffen so be ye catch one young, they's as fond as
ary dog, crawlin' into yer bed, come night, climbin'
on yer lap every time ye set down an' shovin' their
noses in yer face. An' playful! They keeps on a-jokin'
from dawn to dark. But all wild pets has to be let go,
when they is grown, an' 't is matin' time. 'T is agin
nature for 'em to live penned up."

A turn in the stream brought them to an islet.
They went ashore, looked about for snakes and found
none, then sat down behind some bushes. Diah
pointed to the mud bank across the creek. It looked
to him as if the otters had begun to make a new slide
there.

"Iffen 't ain't done yit to their likin', Pompano,
ye'll see 'em fix hit."

He was right about it, to his great delight. Father
Otter emerged from the family den through the
water, climbed briskly to the top of the bank, and
peered down. He saw a stone, or a root, some rough-
ness in the surface imperceptible to the boys from
their station across the creek. Diah nudged his companion, to warn him to watch closely. The big otter
slid down to the section that did not please him, and
dug busily. Out rolled a stone. He swept it to one
side. Next he spied a knobby root cropping into his
sporting ground from the stump of a fallen tree near
by. He tore away the soil with his forepaws until the

annoying knob was wholly uncovered, then he set his
teeth into the wood. The otter is not a born lumber-
jack, like the beaver, but his jaws are powerful and
his teeth sharp and strong. Presently Father Otter had
the knob out. By this time Mother Otter and the children had climbed the bank. All working together,
they soon cleared away the chips, carrying them to
the spot where Father had deposited the knob. Their
last touch was to fill in the holes which he had gouged
in the mud by his activities.

Then the whole family ran down to the water
helter-skelter, plopped in, came out immediately, and
raced dripping to the top of the bank, and slid down,
leaving wet trails on the mud. They hit the stream
with big splashes, rolled over and dived, and sped up
the bank again for another slide. They repeated this
performance over and over again, pressing down the
humpy spots and smoothing the whole to an even surface as slippery as ice by the weight and glide of their
wet bodies.

"They can tote a load of water in their fur,"
Obadiah said, "an' turn dry soil to mud in no time.
Beats all, how they knows as how to make it wet
'nough, an' yit not too wet, to be good an' slippery!"

"I wish I could git a baby otter for Cella, bein'
they're so lovin' like. She says she'll be lonesome for
home things. But mebbe swamp critters wouldn't do
well on the Gulf," Pompano said, as Diah poled the
boat out of the creek.

"We'll be home round milkin' time." Obadiah
measured the slant of rays through the green canopy.
"No," he grinned. "Better catch her a tame fish an'

git her used to Gulf critters! Cella an' me, we kept
pets around till Pappy an' Mammy was nigh franzied.
Ab an' Si, too; like as not, ary night, they'll bring in
some critter. Though they ain't so partial to 'em as
Cella an' me was. But I've larned as how wild is wild;
an' ye can't give ary critter what'll make up to hit
for leavin' hits own woods or water.

"Take dur, now. A little young dur is purty an'
sweet. But hit grows to a buck with antlers. An',
come fall, hits neck swells turrible, an' hit's all in a
franzy to get hitself a she-un, an' chargin' other males
to fit to the death. Hit mebbe follered ye around,
gentle as a calf, all summer. But, come fall, hit'll go
for ye, an' strike ye down with hits forefeet, jest like
ye was a enemy.

"B'ar cubs, otters, birds, dur, we've had 'em all.
'Pears like I can't nuvver spend 'nough time a-studyin' on 'em. But I've larned as how humans is humans,
an' critters is critters; an' the critters, too, has got
their own kind of self-respect an' their own laws an'
ways of livin'. Wild is wild."

The run carried the boat into a wide prairie
ringed with pine and hardwoods. Above, the autumn
sun shone from a clear blue expanse; there were no
cypresses to shut out the sky. Obadiah had a duck-
blind here. He slipped the boat in behind it, explain-
ing to Pompano that it was one of his favorite places
for a-studyin' on critters because here he could observe the wild life of both the prairies and the piney
woods. And it was a great place for birds.

Thousands of wings were spread upon the brilliant sky: acres of birds, twisting, turning, floating

in flocks—wood ducks, white ibis and wood ibis.
Ward's herons, little blue herons with long dark green
crests on their odd, receding heads and pointed feathers between their grayish green shoulders, and night
herons with yellow crests. Huge, flapping water turkeys plunged through the water among the reeds and
lily pads; limpkins cried from the woods; and great
sandhill cranes drifted down like shadows.

Obadiah said that he had always been more interested in animals than in birds, until he met a scientist from Ameriky who had something to do with the
bird sanctuary. Hired by this man to take him about,
he had learned enough about birds to want to watch
them himself.

"Womern's hats!" he spat scornfully; "killin' for
food is righteous. But womern's hats!"

He explained that the sanctuary was to save the
egrets, as well as other birds, before they were all
killed off.

"Years ago, so he was a-tellin', the marshes outside was fuller of egrets than Okefenokee is now. The
big white uns an' the little white uns, too. The little
blue heron's young-uns is white, an' looks like egrets,
an' so hunerts of 'em got shot. 'T was turrible! The
law's agin killin' egrets; an' some triflin' feather
hunters tried to git the plumes by cuttin' 'em off the
backs of livin' birds. Sich oneriness! Egrets only wears
plumes when they is nestin'. So, when they was killed
for to deck womern's hats, their young-uns starved
in the nestses. Egrets nests about forty foot from the
ground; an' some is jest startin' to lay eggs whilst
others is hatchin'."

He pointed out a great blue heron standing motionless in the shallows, waiting for its meal to swim up to it. The misty blue coloring of its plumage seemed to blend into both the bank and the reedy

water, so that one needed sharp eyes to see him. That might be why the feather hunters and sportsmen had not killed off herons as well as egrets; they were hard to see. While the boys watched, the heron's long bill came up with a fish. He tossed the silvery flake into the air and caught it, head downwards. " 'T is said as how he alus swallows hit by hits head 'cause, iffen he gulped hit by the tail, the fins would scratch his throat. I dunno."

The wild ducks from the North would be coming in soon. "Thar'll be a mess of 'em in the swamp, come winter, feedin' an' warmin' theirselves in the sun." Black ducks, mallards, widgeons, blue- and green-winged teal, and pintails were common visitors. The only ducks that lived in Okefenokee the year round were the beautiful little wood ducks. He hated to kill them and only did so when he needed them for food. Gators got plenty of them. Instead of building nests on the ground, like other ducks, they made theirs in hollow trees.

"Ye can't be sartin whar they'll nest. Sometimes hit's in a hollow tree five foot from the ground. An' hit might be a good hole fifty or sixty foot high. They is partial to old woodpeckers' holes. The mammy duck lines the nest with down from her breast. Iffen so be they nests low, she carries her young-uns to water in her mouth, one at a time, like a cat carries hits kittens. Iffen the nest is way up high, she carries 'em clingin' on her back, when she flies 'em down to water. Wood ducks is right peart on the wing, best fliers of all the ducks."

He had told all this to another scientist on a visit to the swamp, and been disbelieved. It rankled. "So durn sartin sure hit weren't so, he wouldn't stay around whar they was nestin' an' watch till he seed hit," he said, disgustedly.

"They sure is purty," said Pompano, as a family of the little ducks swam out placidly from under some overhanging branches.

Suddenly and noiselessly, a small, slight Negro boy slipped through the bushes and stood on the brink. He was stripped naked, and carried the remnants of a pair of pants in one hand. After a quick look around for gators, the boy dropped his ragged clothing and slid into the cool water. From the edge of the pool he pulled dozens of deep green lily leaves and set them afloat. Then he turned on his back and let himself sink until only his nose and mouth were above the water among the floating lilies.

Slowly he drifted toward the feeding ducks. The lilies bobbed about, stopped and moved again, like any mobile objects blown aimlessly by the morning breeze; but always, when they stopped, they were closer to the little ducks feeding in the shallows. Once the drake, suspicious, half raised himself from the water and his clear ringing whistle sounded across the prairie; then he decided that the floating leaves were harmless and resumed his meal.

The end came quickly. The Negro floated quietly now among the feeding flock. Two plump hens were within reach of his hands. Suddenly a frightened squawk broke the stillness, and the drake, with a terrified flapping of wings, rose and sped off into the shelter of the hardwood thicket; the young ducks paddled frantically toward shore, but the two hens were nowhere to be seen. They had been jerked beneath the water as surely and as silently as though the bottom of the pool had opened and swallowed them.

"I wouldn't believe a human could do hit," said Pompano. The young Negro reached the bank, picked up his tatters and disappeared into the undergrowth with the two ducks hanging limply from his hands.

"Well, Pompano, longer I live, the more I kin larn." Obadiah shook his head in wonder. " 'Pears like I could watch gators pullin' down critters all my life an', lessen I seed yon Negro catch his dinner, I wouldn't know rightly how to catch a squealer, like he done. I 'spects he thanked Mister Gator, proper. Reckon he's poor as a picked bone: hain't got ary gun nor weepons a-tall. An' like as not no matches nuther to make a fire an' cook. He'll et his ducks raw, like a gator."

CHAPTER TWELVE

Cella's Wedding Day

ELLA'S wedding day dawned bright and clear. All through December the days had been cold, but now a spell of warm weather had set in. The sun was warm on the backs of the hunters as they moved swiftly through Okefenokee, looking for big bronze wild turkeys to roast for Old Christmas dinner.

They had celebrated Christmas with frolics and songs and stories. As Obadiah walked through the piney woods this sunshiny morning he was a-studyin' on this business of Old Christmas, and his gran'paw's insistence on their celebrating it, as well as Cella's wedding. "Say, pappy," he jumped nimbly from a soft marshy spot to a dry tuft of marsh grass, "what is Ole Christmas?"

Freeman sat down on a log to rest. "Hit's this a-way," he explained. "Your gre'-gre'-gran'paw was a master hand at keepin' up things like they used to do in that fureen land called England. Twelve days after the birth of Christ, some say, the Wise Men—three kings, they was—fust seed him; this were the sixth day of January. Some fowkses, they say, calls hit Ole Christmas, but most fowkses calls hit Twelfth-night. An' everybody used to feast an' frolic over the whole time from December twenty-fifth to January sixth—like we-uns be goin' to do, provided we git arythin' to feast on!" He sprang up and strode off into the woods.

Obadiah followed his father, walking slowly and carefully now, so as not to disturb the feeding flocks of turkeys, which were much more wary than in the olden days.

> Turkeys, carps, hops, pickerel and beer,
> Came into England all in one year,

he chanted under his breath. Gre'-gre'-gran'paw said that rhyme was made up away back in 1524; and he thought wild turkeys were taken to England and tamed long before they knew anything about to-bacco, or lots of other good things from this coun-try. How did turkeys get their names? he wondered. Was it because they gobbled "turk, turk, turk" all the time? He would have to ask Gran'paw.

On their way home, laden down with the plump birds, Freeman was silent, thinking of far Ameriky to which his Cella would soon be going. Obadiah, sensing something of the way his father felt, tried to cheer him.

"Pappy, listen," he said, grinning. He sang him a new song, one he had heard recently at a neighbor's frolic, all about the Georgy piney woods peddler, who was alus tradin' things. First he swapped off his wife for a horse, then the horse for a cow, an' the cow for a mule, an' the mule for a dog, an' the dog for a cat, an' the cat for a mouse, an'

> Then I traded my mouse for a blind ole mole,
> An' the doggone thing ran straight for a hole,
> With a wing, wang, waddle
> An' a great big straddle
> And a Jack-fair-faddle.
> It's a long way home!

2

Manthy was in her glory. Great roasts of venison, beef, bear, pork, and mutton—the latter a costly meat, for sheep were scarce in the swamp country—were roasting gloriously in the tin "kitchens" over the open fires in the yard. The tin kitchen was a boxlike affair, open to the blaze on one side, with iron spits run through it on which the roasts were skewered. The meats were turned over and over by means of a crank at one end. This job, and that of basting with hot grease, had been given to Silas, who rebelled loudly but without avail at this womern's work. A thick soup, made from the fish heads and thickened with hominy, simmered in one large pot; another big kettle was being filled with the chopped livers, hearts, and sweetbreads of the sheep. Later, onions, potatoes, and seasonings would be added, and then the savory mixture would be fried as a hash. Strings of sausages packed in the innards of the butchered pigs, and a dozen dressed ducks, could just find place on the long table, which was piled high with great golden sweet potatoes, yellow onions, dried red peppers, and all sorts of canned and preserved fruits, and sweet and sour pickles.

Rice and corn meal were prepared, ready to be made into a rich liver pudding. Among the preserves none was tastier than the bittersweet jelly—clear and golden—made from wild crabapples, an accompaniment to roast pork and venison that has no honest substitute. In the springhouse the Christmas cakes waited in the cool darkness, heavy with the scent of the scuppernong wine that had been poured liberally over their flaky golden crusts. This day Manthy would show the neighbors how she and Freeman gave their girl away.

Nothing was too good for this wedding! The dining table was spread with the choicest of the family heirlooms, taken from the big cypress chest: silver spoons, bone-handled knives and forks, and the fine old homespun table linens and towels, reserved always for great occasions. The floor had been scoured until it was white. Christmas greens were fastened everywhere, their woodsy smell mingling with the smoke of the slow-burning fire in the fireplace. A great tree stood in the corner, glittering with bits of bright paper, popcorn strung on long cords, sweet gum seeds, pine cones, and a bright star of tinsel that Pompano Joe had brought as a present from the coast. Holly, laden with scarlet berries, and mistletoe were everywhere. Urged on by Obadiah's voice, the ox dragged the huge backlog of hickory across the yard, for the Old Christmas fire.

3

So the day passed. Evening came; and in the presence of the smiling neighbors, the outland preacher said the words that married Cella and Pompano. She stood slim and proud and straight in her boughten dress of white, with Gre'-gre'-gran'maw's weddin' veil, yellowed with age, bound to her head by a wreath of orange blossoms, Pompano's gift to his bride.

After the handshaking and well-wishing, they feasted on the spread proud Manthy had prepared.

"Pappy's weighted down 'cause Cella's goin' so far from home," Obadiah thought. "He alus set a store by Cella."

He caught Freeman's eye, grinned, and called to him. "Pappy, iffen Cella hadn't wed with Pompano, she might have gone with a no-account piney woods boy." Freeman laughed.

"Come on, mens!" he shouted. "Tune up, Old Fiddler. The 'Piney Woods Ballad.'" The crowd laughed and began to stamp their feet. Freeman led the singing. The guests joined in on the third and fourth lines of the stanzas, and swelled their voices to a grand fortissimo with the one-line refrain.

Come all ye swamp gals an' listen to my noise,
Don' be courted by the piney woods boys;
For iffen ye marry 'em yer po'tion will be
Cawnbread an' bacon—that's all ye'll ever see.

Say! don' let the hoecake git too brown!

When ye go to the cowpen ye must milk in a gourd,
Set it in the corner, kiver it with a board:
That is the way of the piney woods race;
They're lazy an' shiftless an' alus a disgrace.

If ye go a-courtin', they'll set ye in a chur
An' fust thing they ask is, 'Kin ye kill a dur.'
They wear great big hats an' little bits of brims
All trussed round with pieces of strin's.

Say! don' let the hoecake git too brown!

CHAPTER THIRTEEN

Goliath and the B'ar

THE light was dim in the cabin even though two kerosene lamps stood on the shelf above the fireplace. Their chimneys danced a jig with the force of the gale that swept out of the north. The icy wind howled down the flue, sending clouds of smoke and ashes into the room. Bare branches knocked against the uncurtained windows, and black creek waters made talking sounds as they hurried past on their way to the swamp.

It was good to be indoors; better than plodding

along lonely flatwoods trails. Old Fiddler settled himself comfortably in his chair, and stroked his fiddle into a gay old tune:

> She's got cheeks like a cherry, red like a rose,
> How I love my darlin' God A'mighty knows.
> But if I git married, I hain't my own man.
> I'll have to fleech her jest as much as I can.
>
> I wouldn't trade a kiss from my dear honey's lips
> For all the gold in the old Mississipps.
> But I can't go a-huntin', or live my own life,
> If I give up my freedom to git me a wife.

Awakened by the song, the lean hounds, Scavenger and Brisket, stirred and stretched, opened their eyes, blinked lazily, and relaxed again in the warmth. Behind them was a hard day's work, well done: three deer hung from the crossbeam. Old Fiddler cocked an eye aloft—venison steak was worth singing for, any time.

Under Freeman's and Obadiah's skillful hands the wet skin peeled down smoothly from the meat. The hide off, they quartered the carcass and saved a few choice entrails for the hounds. Diah slipped a morsel into the mouth of his own pet dog, Blockie, who, as usual, was lying against him, as close as he could get. Deer meat cubed, seasoned, and pressed into tins, then steamed for hours until it was a tender mass in a thick jelly of its own juice, was a feast for the gods. If a little melted tallow was run over the tops of the tins, to seal them, the meat would keep all winter. Freeman had a special reason for putting up a large supply of deer meat this season, for Cella would soon accompany her husband to the outland.

"The coast hain't ary place for womernfowkses,"
he thought, angrily. "What with toughs full of corn,
an' rippits an' killin's, an' outlandish vittles, an' nary
soul to come set an' wish her well, the little-un will
need shocks of things from home. Cella's the power-
fulest young-un for dur meat."

Soon Manthy put a large juicy steak to sizzle
over the fire. Grease snapped and sputtered in the
pan, and a few spatters of hot fat struck the blazing
logs. In the sudden flare, the faces of father and son
sprang into sharp relief against their long black hair:
faces strangely alike, lean and weather-beaten, with
glittering eyes—and tobacco juice staining their
grow-and-be-damned whiskers.

The hounds pricked up their ears. Scavenger
padded over to the door and whined softly. A clear,
long-drawn cry was heard above the rush of the
wind. "Sounds like Absalom a-hollerin'." Obadiah
dropped another morsel into Blockie's mouth. "An'
Silas will likely be a-snuddin' for his supper."

The door banged open to let in the stinging air
and a whirl of dead leaves with the two boys. They
lugged a small Florida bear after them, its legs tied to
a long sapling. Their father looked up and sniffed disapprovingly. "Best ye could do? Great catawumpus!
I remember when yer gran'paw kilt two hunert big
fellers every season. Whar'd ye git this a-one?"

"Down nigh Mis' Claramond's bee gums." Absalom slid a rope around the bear's hind legs and
pulled it up to the crossbeam. "Mis' Claramond, she
reckons he's bin a-stealin' her wild honey."

"Got a nice passel o' fur." Freeman ran a hand through the thick dark hair. "Oh, Lawsy! Lawsy! He's all shot to pieces! How come he's got so many holes?"

Silas grinned. "Ab got him the fust time, but he rared up an' kept a-comin'. Took five shots to down him."

"Huh," his father snorted. "Guess we better call Ab a five-shot scoggin! I remember my pappy sayin' it was a waste of good lead to use it on a b'ar. Pompano, I reckon ye nuvver heerd tell about David, an' his brother Goliath, the greatest hunter in the swamp? Nor the awful end Goliath come to— through sinful waste? Well, pull up, all of ye, an' fill yer plateses afore ye mummick the gaston juice of yer stomachs, an' I'll see can I call up 'nough larnin' to tell.

"Way back," he began, "long afore we-uns was borneded, two brothers, David and Goliath, took for themselves a passel of land nighabout the swamp. Ye'd a-thought they'd a-bin lonesome like, havin' fit in the Civil War whar they alus had lotsa company, an' all; but no, after the din of battle they liked the peace an' quiet—leastways, that's the way they was a-tellin'.

"The swamp hereabout, moren out yon in Ameriky, was full o' varmints. They was thick as niggers playin' hop-an'-go-fetch-hit in a melon patch. Mink, otter, an' foxes was so crowded in the nestses they jest spilled over the edge; an' wolves a-howlin', an' painters meowlin', kept fowkses awake nights.

Howsomever, livin' bein' so easy come by, David an' Goliath settled down to stay.

"They do tell as how their maw, bein' Scotch, were blessed with second sight, an' nary named the boys till she got her sign. It were a long time a-comin'. But one dark night, when she rolled the bed, a-worrin', a bright cloud 'peared outside her window; an' on hit, writ in letters of fire, was the names, David an' Goliath. So she called the littlest 'un David, an' she called the big 'un Goliath; but they never fit, like in the Bible. They alus stuck togither tightern the bark on a swamp hickory afore sap-runnin' time. David were the smart one—little an' spry. He had lotsa book larnin', but a rookus agin womern. Goliath, he were big like a giant, an' slow, but the best shot in the swamp. He couldn't read ary word, but he got hisself a couthy woman—three in all, he had— to share his homesite. Twenty-two children was born in their image. All grew up safe an' well, 'ceptin' one, as was et by a gator, accidental.

"Goliath farmed it some, but he was a great hand to hunt and fish. He could call all the birds by their fust names. An', Plant Woman, ye'll be interested to hear as how he alus remembered the right kinds of bark to brew up for hereditation of the liver. I've heerd tell, often an' often, how he'd go to the mounds whar the ole giants is buried, an' hunt for cookin' pots and weepons they'd used. Fowkses wondered how he dast. '*I hain't skeered of nothin'!*' he'd say. An' every season, when the fur was good and thick, he'd kill hisself about two hunert b'ars. Nobody in those days ever bothered with little 'uns like ye got,

Ab, with yer plumb waste of lead. Most b'ars they kilt weighted upwards of four hunert pounds.

"One night, come middlin' dark, he was follerin' a cowpath home. He'd bin out smokin' a wild bee gum, needin' some long sweetnin'. Well, he heerd somethin' gruntin' a-back of some gallberry bushes; an', thinks he, 'iffen that's a nice young razorback, I'll be a-takin' hit home with me.' He eased through the brush an' nigh skipped a beat in his breathin' at what he saw. Thar was poor David, flat as a hoecake, with a big *b'ar* a-standin' over him! Hit were snarlin' in his face an' all set to claw an' chaw him to bits. Course, goin' on a peaceable passel o' work as he done, Goliath had no weepon to hand, only his bee ax. But, knowin' the ways of wild things, he jest took the honeypot an' turned it upside down on the ground. That b'ar, he whined like a ole houn' that smells a nice juicy dur bone. Thar was no resistin' that mess of sweetness. He stepped offen David an' nosed into hit. While the b'ar was a-guzzlin' the long sweetnin', Goliath swung the ax down hard an' hit him in the head. 'T is said the b'ar rared straight up, like a man, an' fit an' fit, but he warn't no match for Goliath. Goliath'd swing the ax an' down would go the b'ar, then up he'd come agin an' swing his big claws at Goliath. But at last he give up an' dropped. After Goliath knocked the b'ar down, he stomped an' stomped on him, like as if he war possessed by demons. He went mighty nigh crazy at the end.

"Hit took a while, but at last David got him home, an' quieted. But he were nuvver the same agin. Ye see, all those years an' years he'd bin gittin' his b'ars with good lead bullets; an', him bein' Scotch, sich sinful waste preyed on his mind. Alus after that, Goliath hunted his b'ars with a pot of long sweetnin' an' a bee ax.

"After he died his speret couldn't rest. Come night, they tell, he walked in the swamp a-hollerin' an' a-hollerin', an' a-darin' the b'ars to come out an' fit. My pappy seed him often, in the dark o' the moon."

CHAPTER FOURTEEN

Diah on Lost Island

S TILLNESS hung over the little clearing by the side of the lagoon. The only visible motion was silent —a buzzard soaring above the island. Diah shivered as the winged shadow swept across the water. "Hit be the quiet," he decided, tilting back his head to watch the bird's flight. The late afternoon light shone clearly on the vulture's naked, crimson head and spreading wings of dusky black.

164

The pond, not more than fifty feet across and about two hundred yards long, was merely an extension of the run, hardly wider than his boat, which Diah had followed from the marsh. Large pines, their branches fringed with blackish green needles, and a few gum and water oaks grew down to its banks. No lily pads floated on the dark water, and no reeds grew along the shore. Not a fish splashed, not a frog croaked. "Water must be plenty deep," Diah reflected as he filled his coffeepot. "Whole place hain't natural. Hain't no flowers, hain't no birds, hain't no snakeses, nuther." He climbed up the muddy bank and peered around uneasily. The silver moss grew longer and thicker here, he noted, than anywhere he had seen it except in the depths of cypress bays. The air seemed heavy, stagnant.

Although sundown was two hours away, he set about his preparations for the night. "Bein' so warm like, won't need a big fire," he thought, striking a light under some dry pine knobs to cook his bear steaks and coffee. He skewered long strips of the red flesh on a gum sapling and stuck the butt of the sapling in the ground at an angle, so that the meat would broil evenly from all sides. He had eaten nothing since morning, and was ravenously hungry.

Blockie pressed close against his legs and whined uneasily. He gave the puppy a reassuring pat, and then ordered him to lie down by his dignified father, Scavenger, the best bearhound in the country. "Guard, boy," he told the big dog. Scavenger obediently crouched close to the carcass of the bear, which was piled at the foot of a water oak. Diah glanced at the low-growing branches; it would be easy to hoist the meat up to them later, out of the way of preying animals. "Scavenger acts queer," he thought, for he noticed that the dog held his head up steadily, sniffing at the air and staring into the depth of the forest. He picked up his gun and broke it open, to make certain that it was loaded.

This island was strange to him, and as yet he had seen no familiar animal signs. It appeared barren of life, but he knew that the jungle was always deceptive, its dense bush and hanging moss affording shelter for many creatures whose presence no eye could detect. The thought came to him that this might even be the famous Lost Island, said to have been a Seminole hideaway in the wars and, afterwards, a sanctuary for moonshiners and criminals. Long ago, a Scotch trapper had discovered the old Indian trail to the island; but he was too canny to lead others to his new fur grounds. No one had ever been able to find the hidden run again. Diah was excited by the idea. He had followed a bear wallow from early morning until midafternoon; then he came up with the animal, a two-year-old male, in a brier thicket and shot it. But he had strayed far on the long chase and was in an unknown part of the swamp. So he poled out of the marsh and glided down the first open run he came to, a long slender thread of current between massed green walls, which had brought him into this deep, narrow lagoon. Tomorrow he would explore the island thoroughly.

During supper he could hear the dogs moving restlessly behind him, but they were too well trained to leave their posts without permission. After eating, he cut chunks of underdone meat for Scavenger and smaller pieces for Blockie, but neither dog ate, although, like himself, they had been long without food. The puppy crouched close beside his master, whimpering in fear, but Scavenger stood stiffly upright, a growl rumbling deep in his throat. "Likely they smells a live b'ar too, some'eres nigh," Diah thought, and tried to quiet them.

The light dimmed gradually as the sun sank toward the west. A queer green mist seeped through the clearing. Selecting a comfortable spot beneath the oak, he placed his gun close at hand and sat down to rest. There would be at least another hour of daylight, and plenty of time to hang up the meat. Suddenly Blockie threw back his head and howled, a long-drawn-out cry of distress. Diah spoke to him sharply; but as he turned he caught a glimpse of a gray body, which faded like a wraith into the smoky background of drooping moss. Scavenger had seen it, too; the thick fur stood up in a line along his back, and he snarled defiance.

And then, before Diah could raise his gun, they were all around him. In his terror, it seemed as though the place swarmed with the ferocious piney woods rooters. Their small cloven hoofs pattered on the dead leaves of the oaks as they came nearer—and, slowly, nearer—held in check by the sight of the savage hound. Instinctively, Diah muttered, "Down, boy," and Blockie crouched motionless behind a protruding root of the tree, frozen with fear.

For a few seconds Diah was unable to realize

that death stared at him from dozens of small, wicked eyes. "Hit's the b'ar meat," he thought mechanically, as the leader of the pack, an old gray boar, moved a pace or two toward him. The beast lowered its massive head so that, even in the dimmer light beneath the trees, he could see plainly the long, raised bristles that covered its powerful high shoulders and sloping, narrow hams. Scavenger quivered in every limb, and a rasping snarl poured steadily from his throat. The boar answered now with hoarse grunts. Its tusks, four keen-edged sickles of gleaming ivory, clicked in challenge until bloody foam dripped from its jaws.

The whole herd pattered closer now, spreading in a wide half circle. Diah felt a dank moisture break out all over him: he was trapped. At his first move the leader of the pack would charge. Its curving tusks would rip open his body as easily as they slit the belly of a deer. The boar took the few mincing steps forward, which always precede the charge. With a wild yell Diah jumped to his feet, just as the vicious beast launched at him. Swift as the boar was, Scavenger was swifter. He flung himself between his master and the rooter, his teeth reaching for the throat-hold which would give him the advantage.

While Scavenger wrestled with the boar, rolling over and over on the ground in a death grapple, Diah swung himself quickly into the low branches of the oak. His breath came in gasps and the gun, which he raised to his shoulder, wavered in his hands. Under his bough a dozen big sows rushed together. Gaunt with hunger, they tore savagely at the bear meat, paying no attention to the fight between the hound and their leader. They were not yet aware of Blockie. The puppy was hidden from their sight by the big root; and they did not scent him because their sense of smell, which is never so keen as that of deer or most other wild animals, was glutted with bear's blood. But the yearling shotes squealed and pranced about the fighters, waiting their chance to be in at the kill.

Diah lowered his gun in despair. He knew he could do no good by shooting. Besides, he had only two extra shells in his pocket; the others were in the boat. There were fully two dozen rooters in the pack, and a shot would only draw their attention to him. Perhaps if he kept very quiet they would forget about him, finish their meal, and go away. He knew hunters who had been treed by rooters for hours. They had been rescued eventually, but no one would come to help him, for no one knew where he was.

All this flashed through his mind in an instant. Scavenger was weakening, his struggles growing less and less. Diah saw a young shote tear one of the hound's long ears from its head. With a hoarse, guttural howl of pain the dog wrenched himself loose from his tormentors and stood, swaying on his feet, his eyes blinded by blood. His neck and shoulders were slashed and bleeding, his remaining ear was cut to ribbons, and blood and froth dripped from his mouth. In the second before they could launch themselves upon him again, he raised his head and looked straight toward the master he could no longer see. Diah's breath tore through him with something like a sob. He threw the gun to his shoulder, sighted, and pulled the trigger. Scavenger dropped, twitched, and was still. The boars sprang upon him, squealing, and the hound disappeared from sight beneath the stamping pack. Diah knew that the rooters would look around soon for more meat to devour. They would find Blockie, unless he took the desperate chance that might save him.

He wedged his gun among the branches, moved cautiously, without shaking the boughs, to a low limb directly above the terrified dog, and dropped noiselessly to the ground behind the tree. Then he caught the puppy up in his hands and threw him, with all his strength, into a wide crotch high above his head. And Blockie, who could always git a idee, clawed frantically for a foothold, and clung trembling to his perch. But, in putting forth all his effort to hoist Blockie to safety, Diah's foot slipped on some rotted leaves and he went down on one knee. The old boar saw him and charged.

Diah flung himself to one side and the boar rushed past. It turned quickly and darted back, its slavering mouth emitting high-pitched squeals of rage; but the instant's delay had given the boy time to pull himself up to the lowest limb. He was safe for a little while; he lay there panting, feeling sick and weak. Blockie whined in the crotch above him. Diah climbed carefully and settled himself against the trunk with the quivering dog draped across his knees. The old boar lunged about in rage at the foot of the tree, but Diah resisted the temptation to use one of the two remaining shells on him.

The clouds above the lagoon had turned to violet; he watched while they faded to mauve, then gray, and darkness began to shut down on the lonely island. The old boars' grunts and squeals must carry a long way, he thought. The females fed more quietly, with less fighting among themselves. He

leaned back wearily against the trunk and closed his eyes. "Starved," he muttered; "that be why no varmints." The marsh near by was filled with gator holes. The rooters must have been penned on the island so long that they had killed or driven off all the small game; even the young pines had been eaten clean away. He knew that piney woods rooters would not willingly cross water so infested with alligators, whose favorite food is pig meat.

Sometime later he opened his eyes; the dark had lightened, and a full moon looked down from the top of a longleaf pine. Diah saw now that a large black log lay near the edge of the water on the opposite bank. The trained swamper thought it was strange—and keerless—that he should not have noticed it before, when he made camp in the last afternoon light. Blockie stiffened suddenly and growled, and Diah forgot the log as he pulled the dog closer, quieted him, and searched the dark with sharp eyes. Before him the forest loomed pitch black. Suddenly, at the edge of the clearing, two reddish lights, spaced far apart, gleamed for an instant, and disappeared. Then two more, of a greenish tint, shone in the shadows, and others came and went, seemingly rising and falling in the dark, until the clearing was ringed with a circle of twin lights—two, four, six, seven pairs, he counted—with the odd red ones spaced farther apart than the others. He heard no sound, although his ears were keen. The short hairs on the back of his neck stood up in fear. "Be hants," he whispered.

The old gray boar had pulled part of the bear's carcass close to the edge of the clearing and was crunching and gnawing at the bones, too busy to notice that the largest of the paired lights had stopped close behind him. Watching, in chill awe of the supernatural visitation, Diah presently discerned the outline of a large black shape with ridged back and long, tapering, plated tail moving into the moonlight. "A gator!" he breathed in excitement and relief, "they hain't hants! They be gators! Lotsa gators! 'Spect they be crossin' the island from hole to hole in the marsh, an' heerd the squealin'." He climbed higher in the tree, with Blockie clutched firmly beneath one arm, the better to watch the battle he knew was to come. "Hope they kill all ye-uns," he ground out vindictively to the rooters. Were the alligators bringing salvation to him and Blockie? Or only another death? He would know soon. He knew already that he would not be treed by the famished swine for days, until he dropped from weakness! At least, he could see a very slim chance for his life now. The moonlight was as bright as day.

Diah was familiar with the methods of alligators hunting on land, but he had never witnessed a hunt like this—with himself, also, as quarry. However awkward their gait, they can travel quickly, he knew. "Een winter couldn't freeze me no colder," he muttered, and gripped the bough tighter. His teeth chattered and he clenched his jaws as the stalk in the moonlight began and the malevolent reddish eyes came nearer, then a little nearer, to the unsuspecting boar. Stealthily, and it seemed to him without making a sound in the grass, the bull gator moved forward on its four bowed legs. Once or twice, during that inexorable advance, the boar raised his head— perhaps the noise of the amphibian's breathing had reached him during the grunting orgy about him— and the gator sank instantly to the floor of the clearing, and the long black body became one with the shadows. The starved boar fed once more, and the gator crept on. The distance lessened rapidly between them. It seemed incredible how swiftly the alligator moved on those stunted legs: twenty feet, eighteen, fourteen, ten, eight. Its head swung up, its mouth opening; the moonlight glinted on a livid

throat and on yellow snaglike teeth for a second before they boomed shut upon the old boar. With a
squeal of pain and terror the boar flung his two hundred pounds to one side, but the resistless jaws
ground together, shearing him apart like paper.

The rooters heard their leader's death cry and
scattered, racing for the shelter of the woods; but the
gators hemmed them in. "Sartin hit's a battle sich-
like no man has seed afore," Diah whispered. The
squeals of the rooters mingled with the arrogant
booming bellow of the bull gator. The female sau-
rians stalked and fought silently, except for the sound
of their breathing—like brief gusts of wind, low
keyed. One young boar, caught by a hind foot,
twisted beneath his captor and drove his sharp tusks
through her throat in a ripping thrust, then swung
around and gashed her side with his tusks, only to be
knocked across the clearing by a smashing blow from
her tail. Again and again the bull gator bellowed his
hoarse challenge.

Blockie was frantic with terror. Diah held him
tight in his arms, feeling his heart pounding so that
it shook the small body. He took off his coat and
wrapped the puppy in it; after a while the warmth
and his soothing mutter had their effect, only an occasional long shudder showing the fear Blockie still
felt.

From his high perch Diah watched the few pigs
that could still move make off into the forest. That
danger, at least, was past. He leaned over and looked
down upon the alligators beneath him. The wounded
female was dragging herself weakly toward the

water; the blood that dripped from her throat left a dark trail behind her. She breathed laboriously as she struggled on. Diah had decided that she would reach the comparative safety of the lagoon, after all, when he noticed that two females and the bull had left their meal and were stalking her in their typical stiff-legged manner. She lashed at them with her tail and tried to threaten them with her jaws, but they gripped her and tore her apart.

Diah heard a loud, long-drawn hiss. He knew that it did not come from the alligators, now feeding on the dismembered female. He lifted his head and looked carefully about him. The moonlight shone full upon the lagoon, which was still and placid. But on the farther bank a long, low shadow stirred. The big log was moving, blending so perfectly with the dark shore that it seemed as though a part of the ground itself had risen on stout, bowed legs and was sliding silently into the silver water, with scarcely a ripple. Only an inky patch was visible on the pool.

It floated slowly toward the island. Three knobs showed above the surface, and then, as it came closer, Diah could see the whole of a big ungainly head. The two knobs at the back of the head were eyes, he knew, and the third was the rounded snout; but aside from knowing that the alligator must be very old and massive, because of the wide space between the eyes, he was unable to guess its length. The flat tail moved smoothly through the water, without ripples. Then the monster heaved itself ponderously upon the bank; water dripped from its gleaming armored back and formed little pools around it.

Diah's eyes bulged in amazement and he clung desperately to the limb. "Must be nigh sixteen foot!" he chattered. Its enormous mouth, pink-lined and filled with yellow snags, yawned wide and emitted a roar that seemed to make the whole island tremble. At the sound the smaller bull whirled, his ridged back arched like a bow. With a snap he shut his mouth to a crooked slit and hurled himself straight toward the invader.

The two heavy bodies struck the ground with smashing force. Diah, clinging to his refuge, felt the stem shake and saw the moon-silvered tips of the forest wave like feathers. A moment afterwards a blow sent the smaller gator crashing against his oak shelter. Insane with rage, the reptile struck blow after blow against the trunk, making the oak quiver and sway, while Diah clutched desperately at the limb and the little dog. If the great saurian joined the other in his attack on the tree, the trunk must surely crack, he thought. Directly below him he could see the savage eyes of the younger bull, gleaming with rage. The fiery red, he knew, was always the color of the bulls' eyes in the mating season, when their temper is more ferocious than at any other time.

Then the giant gator used his plated tail like a scythe. The young bull, unable to stand the force of the cutting strokes, tried to back away, but his enemy waddled forward on bowed legs and grabbed him by one foot. Superior weight told, and slowly the bull dragged his twelve-foot rival to the water's edge, his red eyes gleaming malevolently. The smaller reptile dug into the mud of the bank and bellowed, but still the slow, relentless dragging continued, until with a thunderous splash, which drove the spray high into the air, they fell together into the lagoon.

The female gators had drawn back under the oak, and were calmly finishing their meal, indifferent to the fate of their former lord. In his excitement, Diah forgot his fear, and leaned as far from the tree as he could to see the finish of the battle. He yelled and howled in glee as first one ridged body, then another, broke the surface of the water. "Big ole un's nigh about fifty years," he thought, recalling what the naturalist to whom he had acted as guide had told him. Fifty-six years was the longest time an alligator had been known to live in captivity, he remembered; but the man had said that they might easily live twice as long in a state of nature—nobody really knew. Diah understood, from his own observations, why the big gator had dragged the other to the pool. It was because his cave was beneath the water, and here he would take his prey to soften until he chose to eat it.

Suddenly, out of the churning, spraying water, the smaller head appeared and came up over the rim of the island. The young gator had managed to break away and reach the shore, being quicker in turning than his foe. He was already partly out of the pool, when the other seized him by a foot, tearing the leg nearly from its socket with the fury of his rush.

The old gator pulled the younger bull back under the water and the battle began again. The monster's long tail appeared high above the surface in an arch, rose higher and higher, then sank, and the enormous, yawning jaws appeared and flashed downward again, a second later, with a hollow booming clang as they closed on the other's throat. Diah could see the large piece of whitish, scaly flesh that was ripped from the smaller bull, and the blood pouring from his throat into the swirl of water. The air was heavy with the scent of musk as the torn scent glands gushed out jets of vapor; the smell made Diah feel sick and faint. Once, twice, again the big gator rolled the dying bull over. The victim's flailing tail smote the water in wild, aimless blows; its head rolled back and forth in agony, while from its open jaws came a long, moaning hiss. The huge ~~alligator triumphed~~ and pulled the smaller bull down beneath the surface.

Diah watched the lagoon closely, to see if the fighters would reappear; but the ripples widened and lapped the shore with a gentle sound. It seemed to him that only a few minutes passed before the moon gleamed on still water, and there was silence.

The female gators had remained beneath the oak, eating steadily during the battle. Now they lay at ease in the moonlight near the edge of the pool. Bones and chunks of flesh littered the clearing, but they had had their fill. Presently two black knobs showed above the surface at the far side of the lagoon, and a coughing, snoring bellow of command came to their ears. They rose and slid, almost without a ripple, into the water to join their new master.

Black clouds floated up and hid the moon from view. Diah could hear wind across the marsh beyond the island, like surf beating on the ocean shore, or the roll of a primitive water drum; but here in the pines the air was still. Freeman had told him that the reverberating boom of the wind through the grass was due to the fact that only a thin layer of quaking earth overlay the water beneath. He had listened to it often, as now, from among still branches. But tonight the sound in the grasses, which stretched from the base of the silent woods, seemed unnatural and fearsome, as if an army of hants were drumming underground.

Soon it was dark. The exaltation he had felt in watching the battle faded, and terror came back upon him. The thick enveloping blackness seemed to be hiding something from him, and he could have screamed aloud in fright.

Then from below he heard the soft pad, pad of heavy feet. Around and around they went, until he felt the blood pound in his ears in rhythm with their march. Pad, pad, and then a soft, coughing snuffle, and he knew that a painter was feeding on the gators' leavings. Pad, pad—and the crunch of breaking bones. If he could only see! But in the pitch darkness, he might waste both his shells. It still seemed to him that his one chance of ever reaching his boat again was to keep still. Then the sound ceased; but there came another, which chilled his hair roots—the scratch of claws against the bark of the tree. If he made a move for his gun now the creature would be on him with one bound. He pressed his hand over the muzzle of the little dog snuggled beneath his coat, to prevent its whining. "Lord, could I pray!" Diah thought, but to his fear-stricken mind came only a prayer he had learned years ago from his grandmother. He had remembered it because it was a rhyme:

> Now I lay me down to sleep,
> I pray the Lord my soul to keep.

The scratching sound was louder. Was the panther climbing, or only stretching itself?

> If I should die afore I wake,
> I pray the Lord my soul to take.

Over and over he said the little verse. The scratching ceased. Once he heard the big cat yawn loudly, and a grating, fuzzy sound as its rough tongue licked the coarse hairs of its paws clean. And then it scratched on the bark again. But the animal was not choosing his oak for a lookout tonight. The padding of feet on the leaves presently told him that the painter was going off into the forest. He waited perhaps an hour before he moved from his cramped position.

The island and the lagoon were black, and there was no sound. He slid stiffly from the tree, put the dog down, and pulled on his coat. The air was fetid, sickening! His feet slid on bloody muck and crushed bones.

"In, boy!" Blockie jumped into the boat and Diah followed him. He took up the pole with stiff, awkward fingers and pushed out onto the pond.

He did not know where he was, and he could see nothing; the nearest thing to light in the scene was the polished black surface of the water. But it was the law of the swamp that its waters moved. The boat would drift into the run he had come in by, or another; and with daylight he could find his bearings.

"Iffen yon be Lost Island, Blockie," he said to the dog, which was nosing his arm and whimpering softly with relief, " 't is a fitten name for hit. We-uns don' hanker to see hit agin. Nuvver!"

CHAPTER FIFTEEN

The Dancing Cranes

IT seemed to Obadiah that he had poled for hours, a blind man gliding through the last dark before the dusk of morning. Above the cypress tops the sky was thinning to pale gray. But, beneath it, the forested swampland, and the run that was carrying him he had no idea where, were in dense shadow. The chill air was like a held breath, so still lay the great swamp.

"We-uns got to git along right peart iffen we be goin' to diskiver whar we-uns be," Diah said to the dog. "An' 't is time Blockie an' Diah et, hain't hit?" He would have prayed for light if he had known any more prayers; but he could wait for it. And at last he saw it: the run led into a wide prairie under open sky. A cold gray mist, the color of the first light, hung over the water and wrapped clammily about him. He shivered. "Leastways 't ain't black. I hope we-uns nuvver goes blind."

Diah did not know this prairie; he was still lost. He poled across it and into another narrow run under dense interlacing branches. If the night's camp-site were the Lost Island of legend, it was easy to see as how fowkses lost hit. The runs leading to it were so narrow and so overgrown that the traveler would hardly suspect they were there until they drew his boat in: "Wonder whar we-uns be goin' now, Blockie, 'long these here currents wide as yer nose."

He was famished, and so was the dog. Now that there was a little light Diah peered into the reedy shores of the run for game. He was rewarded in a few moments by the sight of a marsh rabbit asleep in a clump of grass a boat length ahead. He shot it and pulled up beside it, with a warning command to Blockie, who could hardly contain himself at this vision of breakfast. But the training that a swamper's hound has from earliest puppyhood restrained the quivering Blockie from following his master ashore. His nose wrinkled and he stifled a whimper as he watched Diah cut off the rabbit's head and feet, slit the skin of the belly and legs, pull off the hide, extract the entrails, wrap them with the feet and head in the skin—a spring pelt, and valueless—and throw them over his shoulder into the marsh. Diah lifted the fireboard from the bottom of the skiff, set it across the gunwales, and packed it with mud. Next, he gathered some stout dry branches from the berry bushes and came aboard, lighted his fire, and pushed off. Blockie's tail thumped, his eyes burned, and his mouth drooled while he watched Diah put the liver, kidneys, and legs over the flame: these were his portions when rabbits were killed. When they were half cooked, Diah took them off and hung up his own breakfast—the plump back and hindquarters with the back fat—to broil while he fed the ecstatic Blockie. Their meal finished, he scraped the board clean over the side of the boat and poled onward vigorously. Blockie went to sleep.

Thinking back a few hours, Diah rebuked himself now because he had not lighted a fire to guide him through the blackness when he left the island. " 'Pears like we-uns didn't hanker to see nothin' more. Seed 'nough! An' the mud war all slopped up with gator blood, an' smellin' turrible." Still, going it blind wasn't good swamper's caution. He thought, ruefully, that Freeman would have a lot to say when he heard about it!

Midway across the marsh he sighted two tall, topless pines, widely spaced, reaching high above the distant mass of jungle ahead of him. He knew where he was at last, and shouted for joy. The two pines, where eagles nested, were near one boundary of the bird refuge; and the lake at their feet was a favorite haunt of his for bird study. Only last fall he had guided the Plant Woman in there because she wanted to watch cranes, and the whooping sandhills were thick around the lake since the shooting in that area had been stopped. From the lake and across the end of the refuge, a run led into the homeward trail. "We-uns hain't lost," he told Blockie; "we-uns be found!"

He used the paddle now in the deeper water. The boat glided onward swiftly through the white light shed by a white sky. Dawn had come; but it would be an hour yet before the alligators woke and came to the surface and the cottonmouths crawled from their shelters to bask on the cypress knees in the first warm rays. Boughs hung low over the run that took him into the jungle, roots and water plants clutched at the boat on both sides, but he saw no varmints. Bent almost double, he shoved through a winding dark green tunnel into a wider current, which brought him presently to the lake. He came to rest behind a tiny islet crowned with a clump of bushes. Here, invisible, he could observe the curved sandy shores of the lake and wait and watch for the thing he had come to see—the dance of the sandhill cranes.

Blockie raised his head expectantly. Diah motioned him down. "No. Ye-uns keep a-layin' quiet," he said and the dog's head sank back on its paws. Diah's gaze swept the dull green shores and noted a faint lightening along the boughs, indistinct in the dawn. "Spring's a-leafin' early," he thought: buds were already forming on a magnolia close by his islet.

A pile of cloud at the far end of the lake caught

his attention and set him thinking about something that the Plant Woman had told him and Pompano about cranes. Of course, the cranes weren't dancing that day when the three of them had been in here observing bird life, because it was autumn then—not spring and the mating season. "Hit were wunnerful, the way she-uns were a-tellin' of hit. Fowkses as lived hunerts an' hunerts of years ago in a fureen spot, an' made their church-house of white rock as looked jest like dawn clouds when the light begun to tech 'em, the way them over the lake end'll look in a few minutes, whiter with a little shinin' to 'em. An' they danced in their cloud church-house, the way they larned hit from the cranes. Hit were a salubriation in mem'ry of a great hunter an' warrior as has got hisself into a place like Okefenokee—all windin' runs, goin' every crossways—Labyrinth, the fowkses called their swamp. He was in thar without a guide an' all the fowkses believed he were lost for sartin. But he come out! Mayhap he jest drifted, the way a man would drift into the Suwannee iffen so be he were a good shot an' could stand off the critters an' varmints an' git hisself 'nough meat to et all the days hit might take afore the runs brung him to the river. Mayhap too hit were springtime in his swamp an' he seen the sandhills a-dancin' their matin' dance. An' that's how come the fowkses danced like cranes in their cloud church-house, hunerts an' hunerts of years ago, in that fureen spot."

The fact that these dwellers in a foreign land were Greeks had helped to impress on his mind the tale of Theseus and the crane dance at the temple of

Delos, though he had taken the analogy between Okefenokee and the Labyrinth too literally. Pompano Joe knew Greeks; only, he said, they didn't build church-houses of shining cloud-white rock nor dance like cranes down on the Gulf. They were different Greeks. In the outland and foreign places people changed: they took on a new look and new ways. Diah studied on it for a moment or two, but he could make nothing of it. In Okefenokee there was no change. He lived today as Gre'-gre'-gran'paw had lived; and Gre'-gre'-gran'paw was as Adam to him. The primitive swamper had little sense of time, and none of antiquity: hunerts an' hunerts of years really meant to him some time before Gre'-gre'-gran'paw's day; it was a phrase, not a concept.

Under the lightening clouds Delos was near to him, and other things, too, that the Plant Woman had told him about cranes, but which were vaguer in his mind, having neither Pompano's Greeks nor a labyrinthine swamp to fix them there. Bones of cranes found in dirt heaps older than the swamp mounds; cranes living and dancing on the earth before there were men; Indians in Ameriky and other places copying crane dances, dressed in the skins, the heads hanging on their brows; people far off and long ago who held cranes sacred, perhaps just because they were so beautiful when they danced in the mating season. So Pliocene Florida and ancient Greece, Egypt of the Pharaohs, Crees and Siberian Ostyaks, antique Japan, came together in Diah's timeless mind and blended with this morning hour on the lake in the bird sanctuary of Okefenokee.

Suddenly the air above the lake was full of wings. The large sandhill whoopers flew over the water in their disciplined formation and descended with a rustling sound to the shores. Diah counted thirty in all, a dozen on one sandy beach, the rest on the other side. They had chosen the farther end of the lake, where the water narrowed and was shallow and, apparently, food was plentiful. The forest, where it came to the brink, was a dull but distinct green now, but the recesses were filled with indigo and silver-black shadows. Against it, the birds showed misty white. Presently, the twelve flew over and joined the larger group. In both bands there had been two birds standing apart and keeping a lookout while the flock fed. Every so often two other birds took the watch, and the former sentinels ate.

Now they spread out in a line, twenty-eight of them, with two sentinels still on guard. Diah's heart leaped as he saw the large bird at the head of the line step forward and begin to dance. "He-uns is a big feller: head must be nigh to four feet 'bove the ground," he muttered excitedly. "Got a wingspread, likely, up to eighty inches." The crane hopped first on one foot, then on the other, advancing and re-treating a pace on alternate steps, slowly, as a great bird carved in white jade might move, in harmony with the dignity and grace of its perfect lines. A moment more, and it went up into the air with a rush like spray; its wide wings full spread, it whirled rapidly, round and round, pirouetting upon air to an unvoiced lyric rhythm of its own. It descended and stood still, and another stepped forward. So, one by one, the whole flock danced; while, at intervals, two that had already made their rhythmic offering to the spring went on guard, releasing the former sentinels for the dance.

This slow, orderly procession of solo steps and pirouettes was only the first movement of the sand-hills' carnival. Now, as if the unheard andante quickened through variations to a wilder music, and caught spirits subtly in tune and time with each other, the birds danced in couples. Here and there, still, a single crane danced alone, its ecstasy finding outlet in solitary leapings and whirlings into the magical rose light. Morning in the sky had shattered the cloud mass into thin luminous pink flakes and spread them closely on a pale gold expanse. The water, reflecting the sky, took on the look of a tinted silver mirror set in a studded and filagreed frame of new and old greens—from the pale chartreuse of buds just appearing on olive stems to the emerald and more somber hues of the evergreens behind their lacy gray veils of moss. The glamour that heralds sunrise lay for a few moments on lake and shore and very faintly colored the plumage of the dancing flock. Throughout the long period of the dance, in its wilder as well as its statelier measures, two sentinels, standing motionless and silent, with raised heads, kept guard. There was no sound but the beating and eddying of strong wings.

Diah watched, tense with rapture. His eyes burned and he felt a tightness in his throat. He saw sunrays slant upon the lake and looked up, mechanically, into a radiant blue sky. The first music of morning was swelling upward to the light in twitterings and calls from hundreds of birds in the sanctuary.

Presently a gator bellowed above his hole in the marsh outside. The sandhills rose, and Diah could see their colors clearly now that bright daylight dispelled the illusory tints in which dawn had painted them. Whitish underneath, with black legs, their backs, long necks, and wings were a beautiful smoky gray, and their heads were smeared with brick red. They soared; and their bodies moved, like flowing metal, to form the rigid lines of their flight design, which has caused observers to marvel wherever cranes fly. They passed over his hiding place, winging toward the heart of the sanctuary. And as they flew they sounded their shrill, triumphant *Q-r-eer q-r-eer— q-r-eer,* the trumpet notes of the cranes, like no other birdcall in the world.

"We-uns better be a-movin', too," Diah said to Blockie, and patted the dog's head. "Cottonmouths is a-comin' out to sun," he noted presently as he poled down the run leading out of the farther end of the lake. " 'Bout five miles home as a bird flies, Blockie; but seein' as how we-uns' boat hain't no bird, an' the runs be awful windin' like, hit'll be nigh ten miles, mayhap, afore we-uns sees our homesite."

He fell to thinking about the bird refuge. It was a good thing if it did no more than protect the dancing cranes. He would bring the Plant Woman next week, or soon, to watch the sandhills dance, because she was set on a-seein' of hit. The dancing might go on, morning and day's end, whenever they alighted to feed, for a month or more. This was nigh the end of February, and the mating season continued from early January into April. "Sartin, we-uns nuvver shoots 'nother sandhill! Thar's a-plenty b'ar an' dur an' ducks for our stummick." He was resolved now to get a job as ranger in the refuge. "So I kin be a-noticin' critters all day."

A faint sound from far off reached him. He listened, alert. He heard it again and recognized it—the cry of the great horned owl, a nocturnal hunter whose voice is rarely heard in the daytime. "*Hoo-ho-ho-hoo-oo-oo-oo?*" The cry sounded again, the first two notes rapidly, close together, then a slight pause, the third and fourth notes separately, and the last ones high pitched and prolonged with a rising, interrogatory inflection. It was the signal call of the men of his family. His heart leaped to it. Far away at the water's edge of their clearing, Freeman was standing, hands cupped around his mouth, sending out his voice to find and guide his son. Diah wondered how long his father had been signaling. Had he tried to hail him at sunset too? The blood pounded through his body. He rang back the answer with all the power of his lungs. He wanted to be home with Freeman and Ab and Si, and Cella and Manthy, too. And what a tale he would be a-tellin' them! Of the night of horror on Lost Island, of gators fightin', an' the starved boar that would have got him but for Scavenger! The death of Scavenger would hurt them all, only nobody would say much about it; that wasn't their way. They had feared he was dead, since few men who hadn't been trapped ever spent a night alone in the swamp; though Freeman had done it once and come out safely long ago, when he was Diah's age, young an' keerless.

Manthy and Cella were even now getting food ready for him. He felt something surging in him, which couldn't come to shape in thought or words, as he saw the scene ahead. Firelight in the cabin, sun on the clearing. His own folk listening, motionless and silent, while he talked, save perhaps for an occasional brief question from Freeman; their fierce eyes fixed intently on him and drawing him deep into the home again and into their circle of the living.

"Hoo-ho-ho-hoo-oo-oo-oo?"

Diah hooted again, listened to Freeman's altered inflection, and knew that he too had been heard. It was not their voices that reached over the swamp, only echoes; their shouts could not travel so far. But, as they loosed the signal call, it struck upon the water drum of Okefenokee, and the vast resounding surface rolled it on, echo after echo, across the wide miles.

PART TWO
River Folk

CHAPTER SIXTEEN

"Way Down upon the Suwannee River"

THE March sun fell in bright slanting lines across the boat moored at the landing. The day was warm and bright, and an earth-scented breeze rose from the land. Already the gardenia bushes by the river were white with blossoms. Freeman and Pompano stowed away food, blankets, and all the other things that Cella was taking with her to the coast.

195

The Plant Woman ran down the path from the house, her arms filled with extra covers—it would be cold at night on the river. Cella and Pompano had persuaded her to make the trip down the Suwannee with them now, instead of later in the spring as she had planned. But she would leave them at Branford and they would go on alone to Cedar Keys in the Gulf, while she loitered along the river, collecting spring orchids and Negro folklore.

It was a good, flat-bottomed boat, stout and large enough to carry them in comfort—twenty feet long by four feet wide—and the new outboard motor fastened to the stern was the pride of Pompano's heart. The current was swift in the Suwannee, but the motor would be a necessity when they reached the mouth of the river and must enter the Gulf to reach the Keys. Pompano had equipped the boat with a centerboard, for ease in handling. One end of the boat was roofed with palm thatch, to provide a shelter in bad weather.

The farewell words were few and not easily said. One who wanders the globe meets many people from whom it is hard to part. Taking leave of Freeman and Manthy, and the inarticulate poet, Diah, and of the magic of Okefenokee—which was in these individuals, as well as in their dark cypress bays and sunlit, flower-decked prairies—was perhaps the most intense experience among a number of partings in the Plant Woman's roving life.

Cella and Mar'lee wept. Manthy, the comfortable, probably felt a little sad but she was proud of having her daughter married, pleased with Pompano

Joe Portygee, and she looked forward happily to a
family of small Portygees. Cella was entering on a
woman's proper life, in the custody of a good man,
and Manthy saw no room for grief.

"Beint ye a-comin' back, Cella? Beint ye nuvver
a-comin' back, Cella?" her little sister kept repeating.

Mar'lee stood first on one bare brown foot, then
on the other. Tears welled from her big black eyes
even while her heart thumped with excitement over
the grand motorboat, the piles of goods dropping
into it from Freeman's and Diah's arms, and the major thrill of having a sister married to a fureen man
and going away to live in far Ameriky! To what
other twelve-year-old girl in Okefenokee had all that
happened? None! Ab and Si were frankly absorbed
with the boat.

"Take keer of Cella," Freeman said to Pompano.
"Everythin'll be strange like to her at fust."

Pompano's teeth and eyes flashed in his vivid,
appealing smile. "She's my sweet swamp rose, mister.
I aims to keep her bloomin'."

Freeman said a brief good-bye to Cella, his
steady voice betraying nothing of his pain at losing
her. He stood at the water's edge as long as he could
see her and be seen; and she looked back at him with
tear-misted eyes.

"Don' grieve for yer pappy, Honey. Diah knows
he's sore at heart, 'cause Diah alus senses how yer
pappy's feelin'. An' he alus does somethin' to cheer
him," Pompano said. Cella nodded, tried to smile,

and caught her quivering lip with her teeth. "It joys me how Cella loves her folks. Ain't she lovely?" he said to the Plant Woman. His dark eyes were warm.

"Yes, Pompano. She *is* lovely," the Plant Woman agreed. "We'll soon be at Fargo, near the edge of the swamp," she continued. "Perhaps Cella would like to land for a few minutes and look at Stephen Foster's monument." She suggested this to divert Cella's thoughts. "You love to hear Pompano sing 'Way Down upon the Suwannee River,' Cella. Stephen Foster is the man who composed the song—made it up, you know."

"Like swamp fowkses makes up their own songs?" the girl asked, interested at once because here was something new to learn—and the song was one of Pompano's.

"We'll stop awhile an' see him," Pompano said, "if Cella wants."

"Oh, yes!" she answered eagerly, and he beamed. "Brung yer banjo," she commanded blithely, a little later, when he moored the boat near the lonely little station at Okefenokee's southern gateway—just a cluster of houses and the granite shaft.

Cella spelled out the words slowly, while Pompano stood by eying his literate wife with pride:

Erected in Memory of
Stephen Collins Foster
At the Source of the Stream
Which He Made Immortal
in Song

SUWANNEE RIVER

"What d'ye know 'bout he-uns, Plant Woman?" Cella asked later, when they were seated at the base of the shaft. "Whar'bouts were his homesite on the Suwannee?"

"Nowhere, Cella. He was born way out in America in a house overlooking another river, called the Allegheny. He only came south a few times for short visits, and he never saw the Suwannee River which he made so famous."

"How come he sung 'bout it, never seein' it?" Pompano wanted to know.

"He saw the name on a map and thought it beautiful. He had been intending to use the name of another southern river, the Pee Dee, in a song. But when the lovelier word, Suwannee, caught his eye, he forgot all about the other. You sing many of his songs, Pompano, besides 'Old Folks at Home,' which is what he called his Suwannee song: 'My Old Kentucky Home,' 'Old Black Joe,' 'Massa's in de Cold, Cold Ground,' and the air you used to pick on your banjo, with variations of your own, when you courted Cella summer evenings in the clearing."

Pompano's lithe fingers took hold of the strings. While the tale went on he played the theme pianissimo—"Come Where My Love Lies Dreaming." A flush rose in Cella's cheeks her lips parted. Her frank eyes were on him, like blue ixias deepening and brightening with the morning sun.

"Stephen Foster was born in a village called Lawrenceville, in Pennsylvania—that's the name of a state, like Georgia, like Florida. It was the Fourth of July, in the year eighteen hundred and twenty-six, when his mammy found him. There was such a roar going on, cannon booming and drums beating, that his family were terribly frightened about the tiny newborn baby. 'Oh! he'll be deaf! It'll pierce his eardrums! He'll be stone deaf!' they wailed."

Pompano grinned and said that Foster had heard "lotsa tunes for a deaf man." Cella wanted to know if he had any brothers and sisters and was pleased to learn that he was the ninth child in the family and well surrounded with affection: he was the maker of Pompano's songs and her heart opened to him.

Much of Foster's history would have meant nothing to these two young people: his life in cities, his dealings with music publishers and the Christy Minstrels, his marriage and separation, his drinking and the troubles it brought on him in a social world so different from the environs of a moonshiner's still, and his early death. But his joy in melody and his clinging love of his mother and his home, of the happy things of childhood, these were natural and comprehensible to them.

"His best songs, the songs most loved and sung over and over again by his countrymen, have his love of home in them," the Plant Woman concluded as they rose to go. Cella's eyes were wet again.

"I like he-uns for lovin' his fowkses," she said.

Pompano took her hand in his. They walked ahead of the Plant Woman to the boat, his banjo swinging from one hand, his other holding Cella's. He sang to her:

When I was playin' with my brother
Happy was I.
Oh! take me to my kind old mother
There let me live an' die.
All the world am sad an' dreary
Everywhere I roam:
Oh! darkies, how my heart grows weary,
Far from the old folks at home.

The boat slid into the current and moved gaily on its two-hundred-and-forty-mile run to the Gulf.

CHAPTER SEVENTEEN

Florida Jungle

ALL day they floated on the quiet river through swamps and islands of floating weeds. Often the jungle leaned over and closed them in. Cella and the Plant Woman lay, stretched at ease on blankets, in the bottom of the craft, and watched the bright birds and squirrels in the trees. For hours at a time

Pompano cut the motor and they drifted with the slow current; they had no way of measuring the miles they traveled.

Late in the afternoon the boat slid around a sharp bend in the river, where a creek flowed sluggishly down through a small cypress swamp. The two women, who had become drowsy from the gentle rocking motion and the sun on the river, opened their eyes in alarm as the water below the roots of a black gum on the bank swirled and boiled in agitation. The last rays of the sun penetrated the water and gleamed for an instant on a silvery body diving desperately toward the bottom, with a slim dark shape in close pursuit. A struggle was apparently raging beneath the surface, then all was still; the ripples widened and tiny waves lapped the tree roots and broke in scattered foam upon the sandy shore. A sleek, shining head appeared just above the water, two piercing eyes looked all around, and a mink climbed out upon the bank, dragging in its mouth a fair-sized bass. It was a female, probably of last summer's brood, and the light shone full on her, bringing out the beauty of her long, slender body and her dark fur. As she started off up the slope with the fish in her mouth, they could see the spot on her chin and the light markings on her chest against the rich brown of her coat. The Plant Woman sighed as the mink disappeared into the undergrowth; mink were so shy and so wild, it was a rare privilege to see one alive in the open. At sunset they ran ashore on a sandy spit of land, and tied the craft firmly to a stout tree. Pompano lighted a fire and went down the bank looking for a fish pool.

From their smoldering fire a drift of smoke rose toward the green branches above, and Cella exclaimed in disgust as she tried to fan the sparks to a strong blaze. Pompano returned presently, grinning in triumph and holding up three largemouthed bass, popularly known as trout in the South. He squatted down by the fire to dress them for the pan and sang softly to himself as he worked. The listening women smiled at each other.

> Oh, I wish I was a juicy fruit,
> Tra la, tra la!
> A-hangin' on a tree.
> An' every time my darlin' passed,
> Tra la, tra la!
> She'd take a bite of me.

After dinner the fire was coaxed and fed with slivers of dry fatwood, until the damp hardwood logs that Pompano piled on it had caught; once started they would burn most of the night. Cella and the Plant Woman decided to sleep in the boat, and Cella made their bed of quilts and covers, while Pompano cut dozens of pine branches, over which he placed his blankets. The Plant Woman watched with interest as he wove the boughs into a high springy mat, with the butts beneath, toward the ground, leaving only the tops and small stems of the branches exposed. He called the women to help pull the boat higher on the shore, so that they could enjoy the warmth of the fire, for the air was chill now that the sun was gone.

The bright stars shone red, in a patch of jade sky between treetops. Bats flitted in black silhouettes across the luminous green, turning and twisting, wheeling and dipping in their flight. Far off, a prowling cat cried and another answered; a fish, jumping for some flying bug, splashed in the river. Pompano spoke from his bed near the fire. "Jest remembered. Got a birthday tomorrow."

"A birthday!" Cella sat bolt upright. "Why, Pompano! Why—you nuvver!"

"What fun," cried the Plant Woman. "We'll have to make you a birthday cake, Pompano. What else can we do to celebrate?"

"Don' keer so much 'bout no cake, but I'd sure like to go a-huntin'." He looked around at the dense hammock and swamp that stretched away from both sides of the river, as far as the eye could see. "Flushed a whole flock o' partridges, downriver, an' there must be a cypress pond in yonder, 'cause I heerd ducks a-feedin'."

"How about game wardens? I'm not familiar with the game laws of Florida." The Plant Woman knew how the swamp folk felt about the game belonging to them for food; apparently the Gulf folk felt the same way.

"Won't kill no moren we need for food. Be no harm in that." He turned his head suddenly, looking intently at the thick covert near by. The Plant Woman followed his gaze, then touched Cella gently to attract her attention. Two deer stood there, so

still, so perfectly blended into the background of
dead leaves and bushes that it was almost impossible
to see them; only the firelight shining in their eyes
had betrayed them. Their gaze was fixed on the
flames, and they paid no attention to the human beings so close to them.

Pompano made no move to touch the shotgun
at his side. Suddenly the fire snapped and sputtered
and a shower of sparks shot upward; when the glare
died down the deer in the thicket had gone—melted
silently into the darkness.

2

The Plant Woman woke next morning to the
ringing sound of Pompano's ax: he was chopping
fatwood splinters for the breakfast fire. She lay snuggled beneath the covers for a few minutes, watching
the dawn tint the clouds shell pink. A pair of cranes
flew low over the camp, zoomed upward in surprise
at finding living beings in that deserted spot, and
whooped defiance as they vanished over the pines.

Breakfast over, the Plant Woman and Pompano
pushed through the tangle of the thicket and found
themselves in a little open glade. Cella had decided
to stay in camp to bake Pompano a birthday cake,
and their last glimpse of her had been an amusing
one: she was bent double over the side of the boat,
burrowing among the cooking pots for a suitable con-
tainer.

The Plant Woman noticed that spring was further advanced in northern Florida than in Georgia,

though the regions were only a few miles apart. It seemed as though the season were a month ahead, for most of the trees and bushes displayed an almost normal amount of green. Chokeberry bushes and blackberry vines were in full bloom. The path was sprinkled with clusters of flowering sparkleberry and the golden blossoms of yellow jessamine, fallen from the vine-covered thickets. Mistletoe in thick clumps perched on the gums and oaks, and an odd-looking fern had uncurled its fronds on the branch of a lofty pine. A sudden and surprising sight was a venerable gray tree, leafless, completely garlanded from the root to the top with long lilac-hued clusters of Chinese wisteria. The Plant Woman looked about for traces of an old homestead, since the wisteria was an escape from cultivation, but the riot of jungle plants concealed the foundations, if they had ever existed in that particular spot. Bees swarmed about the tree, sipping from the honey-sweet blooms.

The farther they went into the hammock the thicker the undergrowth became. The excessive moisture turned the place into a jungle. The thick muscadine and grape vines, not content to climb over the scrub, ascended the trees, winding around and around; when they reached the top some of them threw out long sprays and transferred to a new host; others dropped straight to the ground, took root, and and then started back up again.

Just as the sun touched the tops of the high trees, Pompano and his companion found themselves suddenly at the edge of the hammock, with marshes stretching before them, mile upon mile. The little

path, which they had followed this far, wavered in
and out of the high marsh grass for a short distance,
and then was lost to sight. Fifty feet away, a large
covey of partridges shot up from the friendly cover
of a small green shrubby thicket. The *whrrr-rr-r* of
the first flock startled Pompano so that his tardy shot
missed; but, when a second large flock broke cover
with a roar, he aimed deliberately and fired twice,
bagging two plump chestnut-brown birds flecked
with black, white, and tawny shades. Quail, commonly called partridges throughout the South, are
very shy and timid. Pompano declared that families
sleep together on the ground in a circle, with their
tails pointing toward the center of the ring and their
heads to the outside, so as to detect the approach of
any foe.

After warning the Plant Woman to look out
for snakes, Pompano wandered off to hunt by himself, and the report of his gun every few minutes
showed how little hunting had been done in this
particular swamp. The woman turned back into the
swamp and, almost under her feet, the ground ex-
ploded with gray, brown, black, and buff birds.
After a few stiff, awkward movements on the wing,
trailing their legs behind them, the woodcocks
alighted, running a short distance and then settling
down among the brown leaves, apparently confident
that their russet-brown plumage would prevent their
being seen.

Even for spring, it was extremely hot in the
hammock. The Plant Woman was bathed in perspiration by the time Pompano returned, a long stick

over his shoulder holding partridges, woodcocks, numerous wild ducks, and one magnificent bronze turkey—food enough, it seemed, for a small army.

As always, when the sun is high in the heavens, life in the jungle hammock was stilled, and there is little or no feeding until later in the afternoon. An osprey sat motionless on a dead limb far above the path, and a buzzard wheeled, slowly, in ever widening circles against the deep blue of the sky—perhaps to spy out his evening meal. The Plant Woman walked ahead, following the almost invisible trail, with Pompano close at her heels. They crossed a little stream, its banks starred with purple and white violets, and pushed through a thicket of azaleas with innumerable pink blooms, vivid as dawn. A slightly broader trail, which seemed more clearly defined, joined the tiny path, and as it also apparently led to the river they struck out briskly on the three-mile walk to camp. Heavy vines dangled from the tall trees in long leafy chains. The woman raised her hand to push a trailing creeper aside, and only Pompano's shout prevented her from grasping a long indigo snake that was sleeping among the vines. At the noise the snake reared upward; its head swayed from side to side, and its forked tongue flickered in and out the better to catch the sound vibrations. The indigo looked so angry, and so comical in its indignation, that, startled as she was, she laughed aloud; the big snake dropped to the ground with a thud and crawled leisurely away into the bushes. "Chicken snake," Pompano said with a delighted grin. "Reckoned ye might be skeered, if it dropped on ye. They're partial to droppin' on folks an' twistin' round their shoulders an' lookin' in their faces. Ain't no harm, but they like to prank a bit."

"Prank," said the Plant Woman, grimly, "is not the right word!"

They returned to find the birthday supper well under way. During their absence Cella had baked the cake in the big skillet. She had made it twice as thick as the usual corn cake, then split it open and spread it thickly with wild plum jam from her home stores. Pompano skinned the smaller birds which he had shot, and Cella broiled them over the fire, not for supper but to be eaten cold the following day. Then Pompano cut up the turkey and Cella boiled it in the big pot, with peppers and onions. As soon as it was tender, she put the breast and legs aside; these were to be rolled in corn meal and fried in deep fat. The rich meat was picked from the turkey, and the broth strained through an old cloth and put over the fire to simmer. Carrots, onions, and wild rice, with the diced turkey meat and a little precious white flour to thicken the broth, made an excellent soup. Dried corn, which she had soaked since early morning in spring water, then heated in bacon fat and seasoned, was served with the turkey. Nuts from Okefenokee's half-wild pecan trees and a glass of scuppernong wine, for a toast to Pompano, ended the birthday dinner.

3

They slept late after the heavy meal, and awoke to a brilliant day. They breakfasted quickly and set

off immediately. Now the river flowed swiftly between high banks covered with trees and flowering
plants, many of them unfamiliar to the swamp-bred
girl. The palms interested her especially, being different from the low-growing saw palmettos of the
swamp country.

She questioned the Plant Woman about the different kinds and learned that the most common palm
in Florida is the cabbage palm, found usually in
groups, often of a hundred or more trees. The early
settlers called this palm the cabbage because of the
tender heart, which they ate as a vegetable. This is
the salad served today as "hearts of palm." The tree
bears immense bunches of flowers in the center of
the crown, among the axils of the drooping, shiny
leaves. Individual blossoms are small and greenish
white, but the gigantic clusters make a marvelous
display in July and August, although scattered blossoms may be found as early as May. The trunk of
the cabbage palm is always studded with the bases
of dead leafstalks; the natives call these leafstalks
bootjacks.

John Bartram wrote that the cabbage palm was
eaten both raw and boiled, and that the long trunks,
when split in two, were used as pipes to carry water
from place to place above ground. He described the
"vegetable" as follows:

. . . here we cut down three tall palms or cabbage trees,
and cut out the top bud, the white tender part . . . of
the great leaves . . . this tender part will be three or four
inches in diameter tapering near a foot, and cuts as white
and tender as a turnip; this they slice into a pot and stew

with water, then when almost tender, they pour some bear's oil into it, and stew it a little longer, when it eats pleasant and more mild than a cabbage. . . . Our hunters frequently ate it raw, and will live upon it several days. . . .

The palm really tastes more like an artichoke than a cabbage.

The Plant Woman wanted to stop a few hours at White Springs, to see the famous glade where Osceola summoned his braves to a council which resulted in the second Seminole war. The spring is now used by people suffering from rheumatism and other illness, and a large pool provides excellent swimming. While they walked about, and drank some of the famous water, the woman told Cella and Pompano the story of Osceola.

"He was the son of Sal Marie, whose name has been given to a little creek that empties into the Suwannee near here. He lived with his mother in Okefenokee, as you know, but after he left home he became very resentful of the attempts of the white settlers to banish the Indians to a reservation in the West.

"One day, when Osceola was lying on his back near the spring, with a little sick baby on his breast, some men who were hunting him found him there, and without waiting for him to put the baby down, shot at him. They missed Osceola, but they killed the baby. The chief escaped into the forest. Weeks later he and his band returned late in the evening and called across the river for the ferryman to bring over the boat. He and his warriors captured the boat, crossed the river, and killed the white people living near the spring—except for two little children, who hid in the weeds near the river. When the soldiers finally arrived, they buried the whites together—two adults and six children—in an old triangular two-wheeled cart. They had no time to dig separate graves. It is said that the grave can be seen still."

"What did they do to Osceola?" Cella's eyes were big and round, with fright and excitement.

"Oh, later he killed two soldiers, General Thompson and Lieutenant Smith, near Fort King. Then he hid in Big Wahoo Swamp on the Withlacoochee; but he was captured and imprisoned at Fort Moultrie, where he died. Osceola National Forest is named for him."

4

Like most sailors or fishermen, Pompano had curiosity, and he had traveled widely over the country. He tied up the boat for hours at a time, while they explored the surrounding territory.

The Plant Woman had hoped to visit some of the marvelous springs which are unique in the Suwannee country, but on this trip they had time only for the famous "sinks." Strange geologic changes have evidently taken place in parts of the country near the river. Underground channels apparently connect many of these sinks, or holes in the ground, with the river, and during floodtimes they partially fill with water. The Plant Woman crawled carefully to the brink of one and peered down, with Pompano hanging on to her boots in case the edge crumbled.

The sink was a small one, not more than five or six feet across, but looked fully fifty feet or more in depth. The sun, shining straight overhead, gleamed on the dark, sullen water at the bottom and the numerous water snakes swimming around and around. They had either been trapped in the sink during high water or had come in from the subterranean river.

The Plant Woman had heard of a large cave-in, with a barn and two trucks disappearing overnight. Pompano said that something similar had occurred some years ago, when a section of the bottom of the Chipola River fell out, and trees that once stood on the riverbanks and in the near-by swamps were submerged until only their tops, covered with streamers of moss, were above the water. People called this section the Dead Lakes, he said.

The river widened as they neared Branford, where the Plant Woman was leaving them for excursions into the Negro settlements and the old plantations. Pompano knew a good guide named Black Ben, and hunted him up to help her. When arrangements were completed to his satisfaction he and Cella started down the Suwannee for the Gulf.

"We-uns'll be a-seein' ye agin afore long," Cella called from the boat.

"Yes, I'll be knocking on your cabin door a few weeks from now."

Next day the Plant Woman started out with Black Ben to look for orchids.

CHAPTER EIGHTEEN

Orchids and Wild Honey

"I DON'T know which is the sweeter—wild orchids or wild honey." The Plant Woman glanced up at her dark-faced guide, Black Ben. He smiled responsively. "He looks like an Indian," she thought, noting the high cheekbones and the arrogant tilt of his head with its thick crop of straight black hair. There seemed little that he had inherited from his white mother, except eyes that were startlingly blue in his brown face; his father had been part Seminole.

"Yes'm, it's sho hard to choose." Black Ben looked at the orchids clustered at the base of the bee tree, then down the creek where great masses of snow-white spikes, knee high, poured their heavy vanilla fragrance on the warm air. Thousands upon thousands of "lady's-tresses" were spread in great clumps of fifty or more over the drowned floor of the savanna. Among them purple marsh violets, or butterworts, swayed on slender stems above rosettes of insect-catching leaves. Along the borders of the marsh crow poison opened tall racemes of tiny lily-like bloom, the older flowers faded in tints of pink and purple beneath the pure white of the flowering buds.

The rising sun silvered the mist, lying ghostly white along the edge of the savanna, where herons fished for their breakfast of frogs and water bugs. A bittern fluttered up from the thick marsh grass and flew weakly over the mist, its neck drawn in and its long yellow legs stiffly extended. The sun showed the pinkish buff breast feathers, barred with golden brown, the neck with the black band on each side, and the brown and gray back.

The woman rose to her feet, her eyes following the flight of the bird. "Bittern," she said absently, watching it drop into the shallows of the creek and begin to feed. "Thunderpump," Ben said. In answer to her look of inquiry he explained that the bird makes a noise like rolling thunder and also pumps up water from small pools, so that it may feed more readily on the fish and frogs. She had often heard the loud booming call of the bittern, but had never known the explanation of the pump. "How does it get the water out of the pool?" she asked.

"Oh, that's easy," he told her with a grave face. "He pumps up the water through a hole in his bill, runs it down an extra intestine, and gets rid of it. See?"

"I see," said the Plant Woman, equally grave. "Isn't it a convenient arrangement?"

Since long before dawn the Plant Woman and Black Ben had been floating down the Suwannee, on their way from Branford to the Gulf. The current was approximately three miles an hour, so they cut the motor and drifted, welcoming the opportunity to see more of the woods and swamps than they could if they proceeded at a faster pace. The river is from one hundred and fifty to three hundred feet wide, until it nears the Gulf. In most places the banks are so steep that there is no shallow water near the shore; hence, comparatively little bird life is to be seen. Water turkeys and buzzards, with a few black vultures, sat in groups on dead trees. Kingfishers flew up and down the river, or perched on stumps a few feet above the water, intently scanning the surface for fish. They are expert fishers, diving quickly beneath the water and reappearing almost instantly with wriggling fish in their bills. In nestingtime they carry the catch to their young in the tunnels which they have dug in the sand of the riverbank. These tunnels are about four inches in diameter and from five to fifteen feet in length. The eggs are white and are laid on the floor, where the mother bird surrounds them, as she broods, with heaps of regurgitated fishbones.

Knowing that the only town of any size between Branford and the Gulf was Old Town, the woman expressed her surprise at the absence of bird life, remarking that she expected to find the heavily wooded sections filled with all kinds. In answer, Black Ben turned the boat into one of the innumerable little creeks that lead off into the sloughs and swamps back of the higher ground along the riverbank.

The bluffs along the river were fairly dry, and the woman decided to explore them before going on up the creek. The young leaves of the deciduous oaks were unfolding, showing delicate tints of salmon pink and green; mixed with oaks were bay, magnolia, sweet gum, red maple, and river birch—the latter a tall tree, sometimes a hundred feet high, with papery, reddish brown bark flaking off in long strips. The undergrowth was so dense she could scarcely force her way through; but the air plants, growing thickly on many of the trees, looked interesting and she pushed on. Spanish moss covered many of the live oaks along the river, and mistletoe perched on trees of various kinds. An immense live oak toward the center of the dry area was literally covered with red and green tillandsias. One kind, a large pale green air plant with long arching leaves that hung down nearly three feet, appeared to be filled with water in the reservoir formed by the dilated leaves at the base of the plant. On climbing up to look into the reservoir the Plant Woman was intrigued by the lovely green and gold occupant, which batted its big eyes at her sleepily and flicked out a red tongue for the insect she offered; later she found that this tree frog was a common resident of such airy pools.

Brilliant green resurrection ferns grew all over the leaning trunks of certain of the live oaks; these ferns dry up and become a dull brown in droughts, but spring into fresh new greens after a rain. The woman remembered seeing the tiny shriveled ferns offered for sale in northern cities. Buy one, take it home and immerse it in water, and all its lovely verdure returns.

On their way back to the creek they crossed a pine bluff where white-eyed towhees and yellow-throats were plentiful among the palmetto scrub· and pinewoods sparrows, almost indistinguishable in the early light, fluttered among the scrub and sang their high-pitched, reedlike notes over and over. Back in the boat, Ben paddled slowly up the winding waterway under the cypress trees. A half mile from the river the creek flowed into the savanna, lush with the richness of spring, and dotted here and there with shallow grassy ponds. Stunted cypresses, singly and in groups, spread along the shores or in the water, and there the Ward's herons had built their nests and were raising their young. Even in the dim light the Plant Woman could see the birds' smoke-gray bodies clearly, with the white line in the middle of the forehead between the black sides of the head. Then the morning came full and the orchids stood forth in all their beauty, and she forgot the herons.

Black Ben, however, decided to have some of the honey from a wild bee tree but agreed to take only what they actually needed, leaving the rest for the golden bees which stood on their heads to sip the nectar from the irises. Thousands of these blue flowers were unfurling their three curved outer petals, and three paler upright ones, over hundreds of acres of the marsh; here and there among the blue were large patches of white iris, swaying with the wind on stems three feet long.

Ben built a smudge fire to stupefy the bees, covered his face with netting, and pulled on a pair of old gloves. From a safe distance the woman watched him chop a small hole in the tree and lay bare the long, pale gold layers of soft comb. He filled two wide-mouthed gourds with the fragrant honey and stowed them away in the boat; the woman decided to take one to Cella, whom she was to visit early the following week.

The Plant Woman's camp supper that evening gave her the first taste of that famous Florida delicacy, the "hush-puppy"—hoecake wrapped around finely chopped onions and fried with fish in a kettle of hot fat. The honey, she discovered, was like the wild honey of the swamp country. "Why do the Negroes and crackers along the river call syrup and molasses long sweetnin'—the same name the swamp folk give to wild honey?" she asked. "Can't rightly say, ma'am," Ben replied. "Jest a custom."

A damp wind from the river carried with it the heavy fragrance of the orchids. Thousands were in bloom, she knew, covering the piney woods, the marshes, and the lowlands with sheets of pink and white and purple; the warm sun of spring would beat down upon them and bees would buzz drowsily from flower to flower. Half asleep, she looked up, startled, to see Ben standing before her with a strange flower in his hand. "Thought you'd like it," he mumbled sheepishly, "seein' as it's a new weed." The woman took it carefully into her hand. "I should say I would," she said, "it's one of the loveliest of all the ground orchids in Florida. It's not so showy as the orchids that grow on trees in the southern part of the state, below the Caloosahatchee River, but just look how beautifully the beard is placed on its lip."

Ben bent his head to look at the delicate pink orchid in her hand. "I'd sure like to know 'bout flowers. Injuns likes flowers. An' white folks does, too. So I gets it both ways."

The Plant Woman looked up at his eager face. "Why, Ben, I didn't know you were interested in plants. Sit down here, and I'll tell you about a few of them. I'll leave you my orchid book, and you can hunt them up later for yourself." She showed him a picture of the orchid in her hand. "This little one, which covers the low grounds along the riverbanks, is called earrings by the children; there are three or four different kinds blooming from winter to mid-summer—some of them are pink, and others are white tinged with purple. Once in a great while you will find one which is almost crimson—you can't mistake them for anything else, as the large showy flowers, sometimes ten or twelve on a spike, always seem to be lifting their faces to the sun. There is another very beautiful orchid which grows along the river, also; it is not so tall as the earrings and it is a much paler pink in color and smells like wood violets. Here it is in the book—look!—the rose pogonia. Only about an inch long, with a bearded lip, the same as the earrings; but—you see?—a little fringe along the edge, too."

"What's this yaller one, ma'am? An' the white flower that looks like it, only white? I've seen 'em along the river," he said, excitedly.

"Oh, yes, of course you have. Those are the yellow and white fringed orchids; the marshes must be covered with their immense spikes of blossoms in summer. Turn over the page a minute. See these here? Don't they look like tiny green and white spiders? That's why people call them spider orchids. They bloom in summer and autumn in the pinelands, or in low ground. Then, in marshy places, a little later in the season, you must search for the white spurred orchid—see, here it is. You'll find it most anywhere in an open wet place, where it gets lots of sun."

"Does all of the orchids grow in the ground? Don' some of 'em grow on trees, along the Suwannee?" Ben's voice sounded disappointed. "And what do they live on, when they grow on a tree?"

The woman settled herself more comfortably. The supper fire was nearly out now. The night was clear and quiet. A belated flock of white ibis, their plumage gleaming against the dark foliage of the trees, flew up the river to their rookery. She watched them until a bend in the stream hid the phantomlike birds from view. "Tree orchids find a little food in the fallen leaves and dirt which collect around their roots, but most of their nourishment comes from the air; that is why so many people call them air plants. They do not hurt the trees on which they grow, and take no food from them—people often miscall orchids parasites, thinking that they are like mistletoe, which forces its roots into the tree and steals food and strength from its sap. One tree-perching orchid grows along the Suwannee, but you probably didn't notice it because it has no thickened stems or pseudobulbs in which to store food, like the orchids in southern Florida. You look carefully on the tree trunks and in the crotches of the live oaks this summer and see if you don't find dense mats of leaves and stems in vivid greens tinged with purple and crimson; the blossoms are small—greenish white smeared with purple tints."

Ben's eyes glistened with interest. "I'll sure hunt for it, thank you, ma'am. Ain't it got no name?"

"Some people call it a butterfly orchid. But there are a great many orchids named for butterflies, because of their fluttering, fragile appearance."

Having once started to talk orchids, the Plant Woman could not stop. She explained, to Ben's great delight, that although the orchids along the Suwannee were beautiful beyond description, the tree orchids of southern Florida were even more so. In answer to his query as to why orchids climbed trees she said that it was probably because at one time all the earth had a warm climate and a great deal of rainfall, so that during the centuries the soil became very rich from decayed leaves and other debris; thus all the trees would grow very large and tall and close together, and the plants on the ground could not get either light or air. Of course, plants like orchids could not live in this perpetual twilight, so they doubtless started working their way up and fastened on the rough bark of tree trunks; then through the ages they gradually changed in form until they no longer needed any food except that which they could get from the air by the aid of their leaves and stems. By doing this the tree orchids saved their lives and were able to increase their kind until now there are at least 7,500 species of orchids, of which probably one third grow on trees.

"What are some of the tree orchids that grow south of the Caloosahatchee River?" Ben wanted to know.

"At least twenty-five different kinds," the woman told him. "Too many to describe to you tonight. If you go into the hammocks along the river, or in the swamps, you look for a big live oak covered with all kinds of air plants and ferns—ferns grow on trees in southern Florida too. Well, on almost any of the trees of that sort you will find the bee swarm orchid. It is a gigantic orchid—why, the flower stalks of one plant may carry two or three hundred lemon-yellow blossoms barred with dusky brown. When it's in flower it looks just like a swarm of wild bees. Then there is another one called the butterfly orchid which has dull green leaves about a foot long and flower stems that are often nine feet in length just covered with olive-green flowers blotched with reddish brown —they look just like bright butterflies when you see them against green leaves. Still another one has great white blossoms that bloom only at night—it is fragrant, like most night-blooming flowers."

"They sound grand. How do folks get to know so much about them, if they only grow in swamps and such places?"

"Because certain people, who are much interested in the flowers you have growing wild here in Florida, hunt especially for them. They don't look only for orchids, of course. Just a few years ago— five, I think it was—a botanist from New York by the name of Dr. John K. Small found a little sky-blue irislike flower, called ixia, that had been lost for almost one hundred and fifty years. It grows right here in the Suwannee country, yet the swamps and pinelands and hammocks are so wild and lonely that nobody found it again in all that time, even though a great many botanists looked for it, because the man who first discovered it, William Bartram, wrote about it in his book of travels, so many years ago. Isn't that interesting?"

Away off in the distance a barred owl called— *hoo-hoo-hoo-ho, ho, to-ho-ah-ah.* The Plant Woman yawned, and watched a flying squirrel plane down gracefully from the high branches of a pine tree. "Here, Ben, you keep the book. But you'd better turn in now, for tomorrow we must start back up the river to the old plantation country."

CHAPTER NINETEEN

How Br'er Rabbit Lost His Tail

THE Plant Woman was very busy. She was seated on a rickety stool in a cabin in the colored quarters of a plantation that had once been rich and vast, learning to make pork pie as it should be made. "What do I do next, Mammy Marcy?" She turned to the amiable, portly Negress for instructions.

"Now yo got all de 'gredients, yo puts 'em together. 'Spect yo better tell 'em off, so yo don' leave any out."

Obediently the Plant Woman read aloud, while Mammy nodded her head in agreement:

> 2 cups cooked pork, finely cubed
> 2 carrots, sliced thin
> 2 cups cooked and cubed potatoes
> 1 dozen oysters
> 2 tablespoons finely minced onions
> 2 tablespoons fat (pork)
> 1 cup thick pork gravy
> 1 bay leaf
> Salt
> Pepper
> Pinch of sage
> Celery leaves
> ½ cup diced celery

"Dat's all, 'cept yo sweet tater biscuits fo de top crust. Now put yo onion in de hot fat an' cook it till it's nice an' brown." She watched this operation critically. "Dat's right. Now put yo pork right in de same pan. Stir it 'round lively, chile, so it don' stick fast to de bottom! Cup of gravy nex'. Keerful, now —add jes a bit of yo oyster juice, so de pie won't be too dry. Put in yo carrots an' cel'ry an' yo seasonin'; soon as dey all bile good drop in de cel'ry leaves an' when de cel'ry an' carrots is soft, add yo taters an' let 'em heat up good. 'Spect yo might put in jes a pecan or two, to smarten the taste."

"We forgot to put in the oysters." The Plant Woman looked up from the cooking dish in dismay.

Mammy Marcy chuckled good-naturedly. "De oysters don' go in till yo is ready to do de bakin'. Ah 'spects it's cooked 'nough by now. Use dese heah lil dishes; dey holds jes 'nough fo' fohr po'tions. Dat makes one dish fo' yo-all an' one dish fo' Ker'sine an' Gas'line."

"Ker'sine and Gas'line? What have they to do with pork pie?" The woman was so amazed that she

almost spilled the hot pie filling which she had begun to pour into deep earthen baking dishes. "They're poison!"

"Dey ain't poison," indignantly, "dey is mah chillun! Twins. Now yo has to put on de sweet tater biscuits," she went on, affably; nothing could annoy her for long. "An' den we'll bake 'em twenty minutes, an' den—*umm, umm!*"

The Plant Woman placed the oysters on the hot filling, six to a dish, and then, following directions, made the biscuits for topping the pie.

1 cup white flour
1 teaspoonful of salt
1 teaspoonful baking powder
½ cup lard
½ cup milk
1 ½ cups hot sweet potato (mashed)

She mixed together flour, baking powder, and salt, and added the lard, cutting it in well with a fork as Mammy Marcy directed. Next she beat the hot sweet potatoes and the milk together into a foamy mass, and poured them into the flour mixture, a little at a time, until the dough was stiff enough to turn onto a floured pie board. She rolled it out until it was a half inch thick and cut it into small squares. These she placed close together on the top of the pie, seven to each dish, and set them in a hot oven to bake. The remaining half dozen biscuits she baked separately, to be eaten hot with wild honey and wild orange marmalade.

Mammy Marcy preferred to watch the pies in the oven herself, so the Plant Woman, who had caught faint echoes of a song through the open door, walked down the sandy road toward the turpentine still. Black Ben was helping old Uncle Jim, Mammy Marcy's man, inspect some new trees to be "cupped."

Turpentine operations extend throughout the piney woods of both Georgia and Florida—mile upon mile of pines cupped for turpentine, with stills located near by. The process of collecting it is simple; it may vary a trifle in different localities, but in general it consists of a skilled axman's chopping away a section of bark and sapwood, about a foot in length. He uses an ax with a curved blade, and the grooves are v-shaped and point downward. Then he drives a small, thin piece of tin, or bent wood, into the groove; this forms a sort of spout and guides the liquid resin as it runs from the wound into a small clay pot. It takes days for one of these "cups" to fill with the sap from the trees. The full pots are emptied into barrels, standing about in the woods, and the barrels are hauled to the stills where the turpentine is extracted by distillation. The residue is allowed to cool and harden, and this is the resin, or rosin, of commerce. Most of it is dark reddish brown. It is graded according to color. The lighter shades are used in varnish; resin is used also in soap, linoleum, and various other commercial products.

The Plant Woman sat on a wheelbarrow, exchanging an occasional word with Uncle Jim. His beaming face, where sheer fun flashed as well as good humor, and his tight thatch of white curls made her think of a woolly lamb gamboling in the springtime: this, is spite of his years and the solemn dignity which he could assume, especially at meeting.

Supper was ready when she got back. And here it seems necessary to affirm what every mature person knows, namely, that there are experiences which cannot be shared. Such as Mammy Marcy's pork pie. The Plant Woman has revealed the makings of that pie to a few women, when her heart was mellow and her soul burgeoned with generosity, and found not one completely kindred spirit among them. "Wasn't it heavy?" most have asked, and, "I think

it's too rich," others have said. Almost all have
thought the pie might be "very nice" or "quite good"
if the mixture were toned down. Leave out, say, the
sweet potatoes from the crust; use less lard, or substitute a less fatty shortening; practically everyone
has rejected the oysters. In our day of canned foods
and artificially heated ovens, apparently we can no
longer expect brave stomachs. The pie was good! Let
that suffice. It is impossible to sell Elysium to timid
digestions.

After supper Mammy washed up, and scoured
the table, so "everybody kin recline on dey elbows
without greasin' dem." This was the hour when Uncle
Jim told stories. Every now and then steps outside
heralded the arrival of some guest important enough
to enter and take a chair or stool, or lounge against
the wall, his glossy black face expectant. Oftener
the steps did not pass the threshold; but one was
aware of listeners close by in the sweet spring dusk.
Uncle Jim took his seat in the chimney corner and
puffed an ancient corncob. Mammy Marcy deposited
her abundance in the big rocker and smiled at the
Plant Woman over the heads of the sleepy twins
cuddled in her broad lap. A profound hush fell on
the cabin and garden, as Uncle Jim put the corncob
aside.

"Years an' years ago all up an' down de river
thar was a whole forest o' trees an' dey was all fust-
class. Leaves looked jes lak ferns, an' all de colored
folks an' animals lived right spang under 'em, in de
shade, peaceable lak. An' dey all talked an' helped
each other. Umm, umm, dat was de life!

"One day Br'er Rabbit stepped crost to de quarters an' he say, perlite lak to a big tree, 'Good mawnin', Sis Coontie.' Dat was de name ob de tree.

" 'Good mawnin', Br'er Rabbit.'

" 'An' how is yo feelin' today, Sis Coontie?'

" 'Right sma't, thank yo, Br'er Rabbit.'

"So dey talked 'bout dis an' dat, an' den Br'er Rabbit say, 'Sis Coontie, would yo do me de favor ob jes shakin' yo shoulders a little, so to shake down a few ob yo nice green leaves fo' which yo has no use?'

" 'Br'er Rabbit,' say Sis Coontie, 'whut fo' yo want any ob mah leaves?'

"Br'er Rabbit say to Sis Coontie, 'Ah'm gointer carry some o' dose leaves to mah ole 'oman, who is feelin' porely, please de Lawd, an' needs greens fo' bilin'.'

"Den Sis Coontie git right uppity an' she say, 'Br'er Rabbit, didn't Ah done 'fuse yo ole 'oman any o' mah leaves las' year? How come yo dast rile me so? None o' yo fambly git any o' mah leaves fo' bilin', ever!'

"Br'er Rabbit was so mad he went straight up to hebben an' stood befo' de Lawd. He said, 'Lawd, Ah come befo' yo mighty mad. Ah want yo should use yo power an' do sumpin' to dat ole Sis Coontie. Ah'm tired of de way she hats us pore folks.'

"An' de Lawd, he say, 'Br'er Rabbit, hush yo mouf! Yo know Sis Coontie am a law-abidin' 'oman, an' never done no high-hattin' nohow.'

" 'Yes, she did too,' say Br'er Rabbit. 'Pay some attention to me, Lawd, an' keep her in her place.'

"So de Lawd he think it ober an' he say, 'Yes, mebbe Sis Coontie had things all her way too long; mebbe she be uppity.' So he up an' makes 'simmons trees an' grows dem right by de quarters, so Br'er Rabbit hab plenty an' don' hab to ax Sis Coontie fo' anythin'.

"Br'er Rabbit sho thought he was smart. An' everybody had 'miration fo' him. But Sis Coontie was mad as mad, an' tore down 'simmons trees, an' houses, an' everythin'. So Br'er Rabbit went right back to de sky an' he say:

" 'Good mawnin', Lawd.'

" 'How yo makin' it, Br'er Rabbit?'

" 'Ah ain't so good, Lawd. Ah ain't got no per-tection a-tall from ole Sis Coontie. She's strikin' down everythin' so we's skeered to walk de earth.'

"De Lawd looked off toward immensity an' thought an' thought. Finely he say, 'Ah never mean fo' her to act so fashion. Yo hop right down to de earth fas' yo kin go, an' Ah'll fix some way so youse all kin live peaceably on de earth.'

"So Br'er Rabbit hopped home fas' he could go an' tole all de varmints de Lawd fix it so Sis Coontie couldn't stomp on 'em no mo, and 'stroy de 'sim-mons trees. An' de next mawnin' when de varmints waked up all de big ole coontie trees was done gone. In de place stood lil low plants jes lak ferns. An' dey roots was good as good to eat when dey is groun' up into flour. So dat's how Br'er Rabbit done got square wid ole Sis Coontie."

Uncle Jim leaned over to shake his finger at the twins, the youngest of many children born to him.

"Time yo chillun in bed. Run long now, while I talks to de missus."

Ker'sine looked up speculatively from the corners of his eyes. "Tell 'bout how Br'er Rabbit los' his tail. Den we go, sho 'nough."

"Ain't yo ever gwine larn respec' fo' yo daddy an' 'bey him?" Mammy Marcy chided while she changed her position to make her twins and herself more comfortable. Uncle Jim began:

"When de flood was, an' all de world was drowned, Ole Nora [Noah] had two of everythin' in de ark. He had two birds, an' two snakes, an' two ducks, an' two rabbits, an' de rabbits had big bushy tails wid long hairs on 'em lak coons. Yo jes never seed a purtier sight dan dem ole rabbits struttin' roun' an' wavin' der great big plumy tails. An' dey was powerful proud of dem tails an' 'mired 'emselves in de lookin' glass every day.

"Ole Nora had a son, Ham, who played de banjo all de day long, jes lak us niggah folks. De flood lasted so long dat Ham played up all de strings on he banjo, an' he grieved somethin' awful 'cause he couldn't make music no mo'. Ole Nora seed how Ham was feelin', an' he studied an' studied on how to do. One mawnin' he jes couldn't stan' it no mo', so he say:

" 'Look heah, Ham. Everywhar Ah turns Ah heahs de echo of yo takin' on wid sorrow. Be's yo mournin' 'cause yo ain't got no music?'

"Ham say, 'Ah sho is, Father Nora. Ah jes don' see how Ah kin stan' it not to raise a tune.'

"Ole Nora he say, 'Well, Ah don' see as how yo

has to worry 'bout dat a-tall. Jes cast yo eye ober in de corner an' look at all dose hairs goin' to waste on dem rabbit tails. Dey takes up too much room, anyhow.'

"Ham ast, 'Yo mean as how Ah should cut offen de tails?'

" 'Sho 'nough,' say Ole Nora. 'But don' cut 'em too close, 'cause dey is lak to unbalance.'

"So Ham sneak up an' cut off de tails, all but a lil nubbin, so dey wouldn't unbalance; an' he made hisself lots an' lots ob strings an' played hisself lots ob tunes. Jes as soon as de rabbits heerd de tunes dey jumped right smack up. An' den dey missed de tails right off; an' looked in de glass; an' dey bin so 'shamed ever since, dey sit down lak an' go hop— hop—hop, so nobody kin see as how dey ain't got no purty tail, no more."

Black Ben appeared at the door, with a lantern. The Plant Woman followed him through the perfumed garden—its beds and trails run wild now—to her own quarters in the old mansion.

CHAPTER TWENTY

The Rose Lady of El Rio

BLACK BEN could make a little extra money in the turpentine woods while the Plant Woman was exploring El Rio plantation. So he went off with Uncle Jim, leaving her to learn the lore of El Rio from old Uncle Remy, a veritable antique in ebony, and his sister, Aunt Sue, a "conjure" woman much revered in the colored community. Youth, in her daily itinerary about the broad acres, was represented

237

by Ker'sine and Gas'line. When the twins were her guides it was topographically interesting to discover how all the trails converged upon the crossroads store with the big jar of barred pink and white candy in its flyspecked window, and the bottles of Cola and cherry phosphate on a counter inside. The twins' capacity for these dainties seemed limitless.

Only seven of El Rio's twelve cabins were occupied. They stood low in the cotton looking forlorn, lonely, and unwanted. Their heavy logs, primly joined by careful hands long ago, were covered with weather-grayed boards; moss and fringing ferns spread green over their sway-backed roofs. From a distance the only signs of life were the long plumes of blue smoke waving from the broad chimneys—not only from the original vents, but through the gaps in their clay chinking made by wind and weather—and the faint sound of singing in the field. The abandoned cabins had a smoke of their own: the gray wings of birds nesting in the cold chimneys. Nearer approach brought the sight of children playing in the yards, hens, a pig or two, and vegetable gardens—a quarter acre fenced in for each family—already lush with spring growth.

Aunt Sue came out of her cabin—its door was painted blue to keep away evil spirits—and motioned her visitor to a bench under an oak.

"De big house sho look sad an' lonesome. Yo 'fraid, sleepin' dar las' night?"

"No, auntie. I didn't see any ghosts."

"Mumm-m. Mus' be yo sleeps lak a log; 'cause dar's a ghost comes to El Rio, jes to de big house.

On'y when de roses blooms. Kinder early yet. But Ah don' rightly know much 'bout her. Dat's Uncle Remy's story an' he sho kin tell it to make de blood cuddle."

"Where is Uncle Remy, auntie? He promised to tell me the story this morning."

"He's lazyin' in de field, an' takin' his after-breakfast nap whilst he's overseein' dem young no-account niggahs doin' deir wuk. Yo jes sun yose'f an' make no mind. He'll be along soon as he gits every-thin' gwine good fo' de day."

The Plant Woman looked across the wide acres to the old mansion, which had been one of the great country homes of the South in the days of glory. Its architecture was typical of the period, the main building being of two stories flanked by lower wings, the front ornamented with four white columns ris-ing from a brick-paved porch. Heavy green shutters barred the double windows beneath the gallery roof and those in the wings, which came down almost to the level of the ground. All the doors were boarded up except the one that led into the room where the Plant Woman slept. Evidently it was kept open for the occasional guest who might come on some errand or other, usually a matter of business concerned with the plantation. Wherever a nest could be tucked in out of the rain, swallows were home-making, and in the four tall brick chimneys, too. The chimneys were crumbling, and the roof sagged and leaked under its moss covering. In the garden the flowers, once blooming sedately in flower beds, had escaped and spread at will, stopped only by the tougher growth of shrubs and creepers that had invaded the lawn.

No ghosts had appeared to her eyes, but a stillness that was ghostly, because of the deceptive sounds which broke it, had environed her first sleep at El Rio. Wings in the chimney at dawn, nibbling rodents in the dark, and, while her candle was aflame, the beating of bats against her shuttered window; and, when the moon poured through the windows at the other side of the house, more bat wings beating on the barred door that separated her quarters from the rest of the mansion.

But El Rio had its true ghost, which did not move on bat wings nor on the little feet of mice. The Plant Woman had only come a few weeks too early to encounter it. So she learned now from Uncle Remy, who hobbled up on his two canes and sat at her other side on the bench. A lovely young ghost, whose heart, in life, had flamed too hotly; vindictive, still seeking vengeance upon that big house, barred and shuttered, its chimneys cold, itself only the visible memory of opulence, only the specter of a home: such was "de Rose Lady ob El Rio."

Time was when El Rio was a busy, bustling plantation. Paddle-wheel steamers puffed up and down the Suwannee, bringing up supplies and taking a load of cotton downstream to be shipped from Cedar Keys to foreign ports. Planters would ride in from their lands to discuss the affairs of the day with the master of El Rio and his lady, Rose. Life was very pleasant.

The day began with colored folk lighting bright fatwood fires on the hearths, and bringing coffee in

delicate porcelain cups, on silver trays, to the bedside.

"Yes, ma'am. Dey was slaves, no denyin'; but
't was long, long ago, when everybody was so happy."

The mistress of the house would descend about
eleven o'clock to preside at the late breakfast. Dinner
was usually served at three in the afternoon, and what
meals these dinners must have been! Turkeys and
chickens, hams, kidneys, beef, from the farms, with
side dishes of quail and other wild fowl; oysters,
shrimps, crabs, and fish, sent by boat from the Gulf!
Cooking was done in the enormous kitchen, detached
from the big house for fire protection, by Mammy,
who reigned there as a queen, directing the young
slave girls in the preparation of meals and the roasting of meats. Huge cranes swung vast kettles filled
with soups, flavored with spices and herbs, over the
fire; Dutch ovens held cakes and pies, which baked
to a fine even brown before the glowing coals; shotes,
deer, and fowl turned on spits over the flames; and
yams, white potatoes, and sometimes eggs were
roasted in the wood ashes. Not only the master's
family ate plentifully; "if anybody see a thin niggah
dat time long ago, he run squealin' 'cause he reckon
he see a speret."

The Rose Lady was young and gay; her husband
was old and tired. Life on the great plantation became monotonous to the lovely Rose, and she entertained on a lavish scale. Each steamer brought guests,
and there was one who stayed for weeks at a time.
"Dey say he never kyar fo' no 'oman till he see de

Rose Lady; but she done conjure him," Aunt Sue put in.

The old master of El Rio was enchanted with his beautiful young bride and showered her with jewels. But she tired of them quickly and left them carelessly about, preferring white roses from her garden to the master's pearls. When he asked her why, she looked at him strangely and said that jewels were always the same, and she loved best the beauty that must perish. And each day the garden by the river grew more beautiful, hedged by sweet-olive trees and crimson-flowered crape myrtles, gleaming like rosy cardinals through the gray moss on the trees. White roses covered all the riverbank, and bees sipped their honey in the sunshine.

And then the Rose Lady, herself, fell in love—with the handsome guest. For a few weeks they wandered among the white roses by the Suwannee, while the mockingbirds sang gaily in the moonlight; but a slave girl, seeking to find favor with the master, told him the tale. He followed them into the garden, and shot and killed the handsome young lover of the Rose Lady. Then he dragged her into a great room with barred windows and kept her a prisoner; and there she pined and died.

They buried her in the garden on the bank of the Suwannee, beneath the white roses. Before she died she swore an oath, by the blood of her murdered lover, that she would return once each year to wreak some ill on the family of the master. So today, in the hauntingly lovely remains of the old garden, when the white roses are in bloom and the mists rise from the water, she is seen at dusk wandering up the path to the old house. The slaves in the quarters go into their cabins and bar their doors. She rattles the shutters of the windows and shakes the doors of the old plantation house, angered because her vengeance is frustrated: no one of the master's blood is within the mansion now; ruin fell on them long ago. Then slowly, her lovely spectral head hanging low, she goes back to the garden, and waits beneath the live oaks for the lover who never comes.

The Plant Woman had spent the day poking about the big plantation and had wandered through the woods into the jungle looking for botanical specimens. She started back about sunset, feeling confident of finding her way to Mammy Marcy's cabin by suppertime. But the trails were confusing and early moonrise found her still out in the woods— with a fairly strong wind rattling the stiff palmettos and adding to her nervousness.

She hurried on, following the trail, which wound around a deep lagoon. Suddenly she realized that a curious sound had taken possession of the night— chanting voices and the boom of drums. Amazed, she stopped on the path to listen. Drums? Along the Suwannee? And then she saw a little trail coming out of the forest from the direction of the tom-toms; and without thinking of danger—of alligators or cottonmouths or panthers, whose pads left great pug marks in the mud around the cabins—she turned and went into the swamp.

The wind, increasing, made the palmetto fronds sound like castanets clicking an accompaniment to the rolling drums and the voices. She was close now and could see a group of people about the high dancing flames of a fire in the jungle clearing. She stepped off the trail into the black ooze of the mire and crept cautiously nearer until she found shelter behind a tree. Now she saw some two dozen Negroes standing, with their bodies apparently touching, in a circle ringing the fire. There must have been an agreed signal, though the woman caught no difference in the beat of the music, for the circle began to move, faster and faster, the hands clapping in perfect time but the feet never leaving the ground, and their shuffling sound seeming to be only one more accompaniment to the drumbeats. The monotonous chant rose louder and higher, on its strange rhythm. The half-nude bodies swayed and bowed and bent in unison:

> Adam an' Eve was a-walkin' in de garden,
> Adam an' Eve was a-walkin' in de garden,
> Adam an' Eve was a-walkin' in de garden,
> Lawd! Ah'm on mah way.

Sometimes a woman would scream and fall to the ground; and the circle would close up and swing on in perfect unison, as though nothing had happened.

> Eve said to Adam—Lawd God is callin',
> Eve said to Adam—Lawd God is callin',
> Eve said to Adam—Lawd God is callin',
> Lawd! Ah'm on mah way.

They broke the circle now and formed a double line. Two men, with flaming fatwood torches, led, and two more men, with drums, followed them. One of the drums was much larger than the other. The woman leaned forward to see what the drummer was using as a stick; she thought it was a leg bone of some animal, probably a cow. The music grew louder, and the Negroes strutted and pranced with the big drum dominating the night. Boom-a-boom, its challenge rolled out; and the people formed the circle again and started up the chant:

> Adam say, Ah hear him, but Ah shame to answer,
> Adam say, Ah hear him, but Ah shame to answer.

The shadows lengthened and writhed in the flickering torchlight, became smaller, merged in a shaking black blotch, and made their own primitive necromancy on the ground.

> Adam say, Ah hear him, but Ah shame to answer,
> Lawd! Ah'm on mah way.

The woman crept back to the trail and hastened on her way to Mammy Marcy's; for the first time in her years of gathering folklore she wished she could forget a song! The thing seemed to be beating inside her head: even the friendly firelight and the comforting food did not banish it. She had come to this part of Florida because she had been told that the colored people of the Suwannee region were the most primitive Negroes anywhere in America today. It seemed to be true, and perhaps the Seminole blood

—which mixed freely with the African when King Nero brought his colony of runaway slaves to this locality—still pulsed in these Negroes' veins with its own rhythm.

CHAPTER TWENTY-ONE

"Old Folks at Home"

THERE was a party in the quarters of a neighboring plantation the next evening. Aunt Sue had taken the Plant Woman out of Mammy Marcy's hands for this occasion, warning her not to be late but stating no hour! The Plant Woman knew, however, that they would need moonlight for their long walk through the woods; so when the silver-white disk rose in the cloudless sky she presented herself at the cabin.

Aunt Sue, she saw, was dressed in all the elegance that fine laundering, including plenty of starch, can give to cotton. The old woman sat in the firelight rocking one of her great-grandchildren to sleep; the

pickaninny blinked drowsily and its dusky little body
bobbed and shone like a bit of polished mahogany
adrift on foam.

Aunt Sue's starched white headkerchief was
folded into three corners and tied with a perky bow
on the side. Her white apron, and the clean well-
stiffened blue cotton dress under it, rustled as she
swayed back and forth.

The Plant Woman sat down on a pine bench
just within the door. Outside the children played
noisily in the warm night, the ragged dresses of the
little black girls swinging against their legs as they
ran to and fro. She could see the twins, Ker'sine and
Gas'line, together as always, with an admiring audience looking at Ker'sine's bruised toe, tied up in a
piece of sacking. Aunt Sue rocked and crooned an
ancient lullaby:

> Bye, mah baby buntin',
> Yo daddy's gone a-huntin'.
> To get a lil rabbit skin,
> To dress mah darlin' chillun in.

She rose and laid her great-grandchild carefully
in the big bed in the corner and covered it with a
gaudy patched quilt. Motioning the Plant Woman
to follow, she left the cabin, first sticking a butcher
knife into the wood above the door, to keep out evil
spirits.

They followed an old causeway across the marsh,
which stretched away to a black line of trees, where
the quarters were. The party was to be big doin's,
and the Plant Woman looked forward to it with

keen anticipation. Aunt Sue dug in her pocket for her clay pipe, lighted it, and limped on ahead, the woman following close on her heels. The moon was brilliant, and the marsh was bathed in its white light. A dark night bird flew across the path in front of them, and the old woman stopped to break two sticks and place them crosswise on the path. "Lawd, have mercy," she muttered, and hurried on.

Although it was warm for so early in spring, a great fire blazed in the open yard before the quarters. Here there were no separate gardens filled with marigolds and sunflowers, as in the quarters' houses of El Rio. The crowd was immense, and many of the Negroes sat outdoors, some of them with their backs against the long two-family cabin where the doings were to be held; the fire was strictly for light, not for warmth. Inside the cabins the light was dim, coming from small kerosene lamps fastened to the wall, with tin reflectors behind them. A bench was put in the place of honor for Aunt Sue, as befitted one of her position—a conjure woman. The Plant Woman sat beside her, sharing her dignities, because, although she was nobody at all, she had been brought by Aunt Sue and was under her protection.

Off to one side great wash boilers filled with food cooked slowly; they were tended by a short, chunky Negress who went from one to the other, stirring with a big iron spoon. Answering the Plant Woman's question, she said that one pot held pigs' feet, another boiling rice, and the largest one was filled with chicken stew, consisting of a little beef, a few shrimp, some scraps of pork, and chicken enough to flavor. "Pindars" (peanuts) were roasting over a low fire; a great kettle of "pore-niggah-candy"—molasses boiled down until it will harden, and filled with peanuts—boiled slowly over another fire. Chitterlings, the entrails of the butchered pig, were ready to be served fried, or stuffed with chopped liver and rice. The people crowded around the pots, filling their tin plates high with the rich, spicy food and washing it down with great gulps of sweetened water or green corn liquor. A cent a plate was the agreed price, and the proceeds were to go toward repairs on the little white church at the crossroads. The Plant Woman stood treat all around, and was in such high favor that she knew the performance put on for her benefit would be the best they could do.

Children's play-acting games came first. The little girls, clean-faced and solemn—and starched—formed in a line, with the boys opposite. A small slim girl with golden skin stepped out of the line and chanted in a high, piping voice:

Hello, Adam! Whar's Eve?

A grave little boy stepped forth, answering:

Out in de garden, pickin' leaves.

All the children stooped to pick up leaves, and pretended to plait them together; and so on, verse after verse, all of them in unison acting out each line:

Whar was Eve when she died?
Sleepin', when she died.
She died when de leaves turned red,

When de leaves turned red in de fall.
Good night, Ah'll remember yo-all
When de leaves turn red in de fall!

After the games one of the prettiest of the older
girls chose a partner and they danced without music
a "social song," with the crowd handpatting and the
leader calling time.

The couple strutted back and forth, pranced on
the corners and turns, and jigged and buck-and-
winged to

Mis' Lou, she love tea,
Mis' Lou, she love candy,
Mis' Lou, she steal mens all aroun'
An' kiss any boy dat am handy!

The dance ended with a hearty smack and much
laughter.

Then the women lined up before the fire and
sang the songs they sing each day at their work:

When Chris' was walkin' here on earth
Some said he was a spy.
He heal de blin' an' raise de dead,
Go thou and prophesy. [Loud shout] Oh! Chillun!

Three fishes an' a loaf of bread
Was all dey was fo' food.
But Chris' he tuk dis lil bit
An' he feed de multitude. [Loud shout] Oh! Chillun!

When the song of the women ended, the men
stepped up, locked their arms over one another's
shoulders, and, without moving their feet, set their

torsos writhing in a hypnotizing motion, back and
forth, back and forth:

> Yo sift de meal an' gimme de husk;
> Yo bake de bread an' gimme de crus';
> Yo bile de pot an' gimme de grease;
> Ole woman, shove over—git over!

At the end of the festival, they called on Uncle
Remy. He sang in his quavering old voice what he
called one of the "ancients," a song loved by his
people of long ago:

> Ah know moonrise, Ah know starrise,
> Ah lay mah body down.
> Ah walk in de moonlight, an' Ah walk in de starlight
> To lay dis body down.
>
> Ah walk in de churchyard, Ah walk in de graveyard
> To lay dis body down.
> Ah lie in de graveyard, Ah stretch out mah arms,
> Ah lay dis body down.
>
> Ah go to mah jedgment in de evening of de day
> When Ah lay mah body down.
> An' mah soul, an' yo soul, will meet in de day,
> When we lay our bodies down.

Now that the time had come to leave the river
and continue her work on the Gulf coast, the Plant
Woman thought regretfully of all the things she had
left undone. She had hoped to make a thorough search
for Chapman's azalea and other rare plants known
once to have been found along the Suwannee, but her
time was gone. Reluctantly she said good-bye to the
people of the plantations and set off down the river

with Black Ben, en route for the Gulf and Pompano and Cella.

They left early in the morning; all day they chugged swiftly downstream, passing through familiar territory. The Plant Woman noticed with surprise the advance in the season since she and Black Ben had gone up the river to the plantations. The cypress trees wore their deepest green, and flocks of wood ducks were nesting in the sloughs. Most of the ducks were feeding on galls from the cypresses; disturbed by the noise of the motor, they flew away, with the drake giving his alarm note, *hoo eek, hoo eek*.

The journey downriver was uneventful. They tied up a few miles below Branford for the night. The next morning they passed the mouth of the Sante Fe just before dawn and noticed that the river bottoms were alive with migratory birds on their way north. Small woodpeckers and warblers were especially plentiful. Hours later they stopped to examine a little waterway that led into the low jungle growth along the banks. A limestone spring bubbled up gaily in a shallow depression; its sides were lined with dark green lacy ferns. Cinnamon ferns were abundant. Fish were swimming about in the spring, and Black Ben entertained the Plant Woman, as they continued on their way, with an account of a trip he made the previous year with friends. They camped above a big spring, in which they swam beneath the ledge into a cave, and were then propelled to the surface of the water by the force with which it emerged from its underground entrance—"an' I sholy was skeered, yes, ma'am." The Plant Woman said she had read that thousands of gallons of water were discharged per minute from many of these springs.

A few miles from the Gulf the river widened

considerably, passing on both sides of Hogg Island; the banks flattened until the land became low marshes with scattered groups of cabbage palms and dwarf mangroves near the river's mouth. In the dark the forks of the river would be difficult to navigate, since the channel was poorly defined. Skirting close to one shore, on a little muddy strip, Black Ben showed the woman the fresh mark of a panther's foot; the animal had doubtless been hunting his dinner and been frightened away by the noise of the motor. In the distance the lights of Cedar Keys glimmered; and, closer at hand, the lighted windows of the tiny settlement on Pompano's island. Only a short stretch of water separated the mouth of the Suwannee from the island.

Cella and Pompano were waiting at the landing. It seemed to the Plant Woman that she had forgotten how lovely the girl was, with her golden skin and flaxen hair. They stumbled up the wooden path to the house, Pompano regaling Black Ben with his account of a recent tussle with a black marlin, and the promise of a hearty meal. Ben was leaving late that night for Cedar Keys, but first he must rest, eat, and meet Pompano's family.

Captain Portygee, a broad swarthy man, stood in the doorway. He was a gruff and hardy fisherman who could hold his own with the Greeks and Cubans, some of the toughest men on water, but the hand he placed on Cella's head was gentle, and his pride in her beauty evident. "We alus want a gal," he told the Plant Woman. "Now we got a real family."

Pompano's mother appeared easygoing. Her dark, kindly eyes shone; the light from the ship's lantern suspended from the roof made purple shadows in her black hair, and golden hoops swung from her ears and picked up red glints from her crimson dress.

The supper was fresh shrimp gumbo, hot and highly spiced, with slabs of brown bread, and black coffee, thick and pungent. Black Ben and the Plant Woman ate until they could eat no more. And then it was time for Ben to leave, and the whole family trooped down to the landing. The Plant Woman watched his boat skim swiftly toward the Keys, round a little wooded isle, and disappear into the night.

PART THREE
Gulf Folk

CHAPTER TWENTY-TWO

At Cedar Keys

THE sun, resembling an immense Florida orange, was just gilding the wave crests of the Gulf when the Plant Woman opened her eyes. She stretched luxuriously, then lay quiet on the sand, contemplating the drooping fronds of the cabbage palms over her and the turquoise sky above them where white gulls wheeled and dipped. She could hear Cella's pet mockingbird singing a greeting to the new day from the house, across the narrow beach. She turned her head and saw the mouth of the Suwannee sparkling in the morning light.

As she scurried up the path in response to the call to breakfast, she noticed Pompano's father busy among his flowers. Captain Portygee was very proud of his garden. He had brought bulbs and seeds from the Antilles and boatloads of soil from the mainland to plant them in; now the tiny plot of ground before his wooden shack was ablaze with exotic blooms.

"This is beautiful, too," the Plant Woman thought, hesitating a moment on the doorstep. "But, oh, how different from the swamp!"

There are only a few islands off the coast, with the exception of Cedar Keys, in this part of the Gulf, and most of them are bare, sandy spots swept by hurricanes and minor storms, and inhabited only by sea birds. By some freak of fate the fishermen's key had suffered little from the elements, so that the palms grew lustily.

A narrow boardwalk ran from the landing to the settlement squatting beneath the trees. The houses —there were only seven, all told—had been painted in bright colors by the homesick Portuguese who settled there years ago. Sun and sea air and time had toned down the blues, pinks, and yellows, except in the case of Pompano's house, which wore a new coat of thin blue paint over the old pink one, so that the walls had a pinkish bloom, like the soft downy fuzz on a peach. Heavy wooden shutters, of the same soft glowing color, hung at the windows, which were glassless, but screened with netting. The woman shivered a little, looking at the storm shutters, as she thought of a hurricane raging around the low, palmetto-roofed cabin. Cella had edged the paths and flower beds with shells; these multicolored sea shells were a new delight to the swamp girl. Flowers bloomed radiantly against the blue walls; long beds of savory herbs grew on each side of the door. At the back of every house fishermen's nets were spread to dry and, early as it was, many of the men were busy repairing yesterday's rents.

Cella set bacon and grits and coffee on the small table beneath the window. The house had only two rooms, but they were neat and clean. The bedroom bunks, built along the wall, were decorated with Cella's bright patchwork quilts; rag rugs covered the rough wooden floor. Two chairs and a small table completed the furnishings. Cella had made curtains for the one window from discarded seines, and dyed the small-meshed material a gay rose pink.

Breakfast over, the women cleaned up hurriedly, knowing that Pompano was anxious to be gone. They could hear him singing down on the beach where he waited for them.

A ship she was rigged and ready for sea—
Windy weather!
And all her sailors were fishes to be—
Stormy weather!
First came the herring, king of the sea—
Windy weather!
He jumped on the poop; I'll be captain, said he—
Stormy weather!
Next came a flat fish, him called a skate—
Windy weather!
If you are the captain, then I'll be mate—
Stormy weather!

The Plant Woman knew this to be a corruption of an old chantey, sung years ago when ships went round the Horn. She had heard different versions of it on tramp ships in many ports.

They ran down to the landing, Cella carrying lunch and the Plant Woman her notebook and camera. Pompano said that he had often tried to explore Hogg Island, but that it was almost impossible to walk over it because it was mainly marsh and very wet, and in some spots bay trees, maples, and black gums grew fairly large, forming a compact jungle-like forest.

Pompano, with his interest in all plant and animal life stimulated since his return from Okefenokee, wanted to run upriver for a few miles to the higher pinelands, and see what kinds of flowers were in bloom. They passed marshes gorgeously decked with bonnets and water hyacinths and turned the boat into a little creek, cut the motor, and tied up to a gallberry shrub, which was in fruit as well as in flower—the fruit black, the blossoms pure white. Other flowers were mint, forming a sea of blue flowers the color of Cella's eyes, and the titi, or buckwheat tree, which covered the low ground for mile after mile with great flower clusters like hills of snow.

"Look," Cella whispered, "what be that bird a-doin'?"

The bird was a loggerhead shrike, smoke gray and black, with white beneath, and it was acting peculiarly. It dropped time and again from a dead stub into the long grass, and came back with an empty bill. "Huntin' somethin' too big for it,"

Pompano said. The three interested observers sat quietly and watched. At last the bird caught its breakfast firmly in its claws and pulled it out of the grass, striking it savagely with hooked bill. "Grass snake," Pompano said, catching sight of the olive-green body, with a golden-bronze stripe down the side, and long tapering tail. "Horn snake," Cella corrected, with the swampers' name for it. "Lizard," said the Plant Woman with a giggle.

They stared at her. "Scuse me, Plant Woman, but it ain't got no legs." Pompano looked triumphant. "And how be hit sometimes has got two tails?" Cella wanted to know. Then they forgot their questions while they watched the shrike drag its limp prey to a thornbush and carefully stick it on a long sharp spine for future use. Part of the snake's tail lay thrashing about in the grass. The Plant Woman had often seen bugs and portions of the small red snakes that live under the bark of trees hanging on thorns and sharp twigs as she traveled down the Suwannee with Ben. But this was the first time she had observed a shrike going through the process of killing his meat and sun-jerking it, so to speak, in the manner of primitive hunters!

"Look," Cella whispered. "Be hit a lizard, ma'am?"

"Yes. It has no legs because it has no use for them, that's all. Furthermore, it has eyelids which are movable, and true snakes do not—when it wants to go to sleep the lower eyelid comes up and covers the eye—the upper one does not move at all. Birds are like that, too. And all those stories you hear about it sticking its tail in trees and poisoning them so that they die, and of breaking its body into little pieces and putting it together again, are false."

"But they do lose their tails, an' get new ones, ma'am." Pompano was polite but stubborn. "Lotsa times I've seen 'em."

"Yes, I know. But the new tail just takes the place of the one the lizard is compelled to give up, in order to escape from an enemy—like the king snake, for instance. And the new tail is shorter, and stubby, and generally of a different color, so that it does look like a horn. That's why Cella called it a horn snake. Sometimes the lizard grows another tail, wherever it is injured, without losing the old one, provided the injury is not too far from the end; then it appears to have two tails, or one forked at the end."

Pompano took a long breath, "If the lizard is broken apart in the middle, it won't get 'nother tail?"

"No. It will die." She turned to Pompano. They were now passing thick, matted jungle growth. "There must be hundreds of snakes in there," she said.

"Sure is." He steered to the center of the stream to avoid an overhanging branch. "Folks do tell there's a volcano in back an' hundreds of snakes live there during the winter, 'cause the ground is so warm. Nobody dast go in. An' there'd be plenty in summer, too."

"A volcano!" the Plant Woman exclaimed. "I'll bet it's a hot spring! Let's go in and see." "No, ma'am," Pompano refused firmly. "Too dangerous." He headed the boat for the Gulf.

The Plant Woman had only a few days to spend on the Gulf this trip, the first of three journeys through the wild and beautiful territory stretching away from the Suwannee, which is still the principal gateway into it. Whoever would travel east or west in this part of Florida must go by boat on the rivers; the only roads run north and south. There was plenty to see, and she saw as much as possible in the brief time, from the decks of Captain Portygee's oyster sloop and the boat of a Greek sponge fisher who spoke no English at all. Pompano and his father showed her where the oysters lived; they were plentiful along the shore and up tidal streams.

"Can't hardly see a young oyster," the Captain said. The juvenile oysters swim about for a few weeks and then attach themselves to the bottom and grow shell houses about them; they develop to a size of from four to six inches in three or four years. They eat tiny sea plants; and other marine creatures, such as conchs, mussels, and drumfish, eat oysters. The drumfish is the oyster fisherman's most aggressive competitor. It may be any size, from three to one hundred and forty pounds. Its head is broad and filled with strong teeth: its jaw goes through an oyster bed like a snowplow through a drift, and the crunching can be heard on the surface for some distance. Big conch shells also are no more work for its teeth than oyster crackers are for ours. It is one of the few fish known to emit sound. As it swims about in the vicinity of the fleet, it makes the drumming noise that has earned it its name; on calm days one can hear it distinctly.

There is still plenty of shrimp fishing from row-boats: not every man has a sloop, like Captain Porty-gee's. The lone fisherman is an expert net thrower. His net is twenty feet in circumference and the edge is weighted with bits of lead. There is a heavy cord about thirty feet long running around the net; this acts like a drawstring in a pouch. The fisherman holds one end of the cord between his teeth—and what teeth those Gulf people have, broad and white and gleaming!—puts the net over one arm, draped in loose folds, takes a fold in each hand, pivots rapidly, and, with all the force of his body in the motion, swings the net into the water. It falls in a circle to the bottom, imprisoning every swimming creature under it. Then he pulls the cord, which converts the net into a mesh bag, and drags in his catch. He? Not only men ride the small boats out to the shrimp grounds. Often the women go out with their husbands; and widows have no other way of support than by the nets. There was one woman close by the path of Captain Portygee's boat, a broad, dusky, young Cuban in a red blouse, her black hair shining in the sunlight like polished jet; her gleaming teeth bit the draw cord, and the strength of an ox was in her sinews as she whirled on her wide brown foot and cast her net twenty feet over the blue water.

Years ago the Cuban sponge gatherers at Cedar Keys and other villages along the Gulf lifted the sponges from the shallows with hooks. Then the Greeks came and introduced a new method: they dived for their sponges. There was dissension, involv-ing fists and knives, between the Cubans allied with the native Floridians, called conches, and the men from Greece; and the Greeks moved off and founded a settlement at Tarpon Springs, which is now the principal sponge market on the Gulf coast. The Plant Woman had not seen sponges lifted from the sea before one of Ulysses' descendants, for hire, took her out to the grounds. Half plant, half animal, sponges have an odd and not specially pleasant look when the divers bring them up on deck. They are shaky, like jelly, and are covered with a dark skin. The skeleton under this skin is the commercial sponge; it is gray and has to be bleached before it goes to market.

To the gay and hospitable Gulf folk a barbecue seemed the only appropriate send-off for the visitor, so on her last day among them the Plant Woman lolled against a cabbage palm and watched, while the islanders dug pits, lighted fires in them, and set every manner of food to cooking. A wild hog, shot by Pompano, hung to roast over the deepest pit. Onions in their skins, wrapped in palm leaves and covered with hot ashes, were in one hole; oysters on layers of seaweed, on hot stones, buried in sand, ducks that had soaked in red wine and peppers, in other pits, chicken stewed in coconut milk, chicken seared quickly to keep in the juices, then turned slowly over an open fire and basted with a sauce made of tomatoes, red peppers, onion juice, bay leaf, lime juice, and a dash of chili powder—these were also on the menu. And there was a fish chowder so delectable that the visitor begged the recipe from the smiling fisherwoman who set a dish of it before her, and recorded the ingredients then and there in her ubiquitous notebook:

Skin and bone two or three kinds of fish. Cut them up and fry them in oil until they are a golden brown. Add an onion, chopped small, two cups of oysters, minced, half a dozen tomatoes, two hot red peppers, and three cups of oyster juice. Stew for half an hour; then turn it into a deep pot and add six or eight cups of water (to make a large chowder); add salt to taste, a bay leaf, a pinch of thyme, and a dash of curry and serve it with "yellow bread"—i.e., corn meal or johnny cake.

Coffee and red wine went round with the food. Presently the Plant Woman asked a question about storms on the Gulf. Captain Portygee admitted that bad blows, and hurricanes too, struck the waters, which today looked as blue and peaceful as the heavens; but, he said, few fishermen were lost even in the worst gales because of the *Lura Lou*.

The Plant Woman leaned forward. "What is the *Lura Lou?*" she asked eagerly.

"*Lura Lou* is a phantom ship," Pompano explained. "She comes alus in time of very bad storm when there is great danger to fishermen out there. The *Lura Lou* calms the water round the fishing boats and brings them safe to port."

"Do you mean that, even in a hurricane, this ghost ship appears and there is calm water around the boats?"

"Dat's right." Captain Portygee nodded his head sagely. "No matter how hard wind blow, soon as

Luck an' *Lura Lou* come, water she calm down an' boats ride home."

"But, if you were in the center of a hurricane, there would be a calm, anyway," said the Plant Woman, thinking that might be what they meant, although the center of such a storm is no place any sailor would be from choice.

"No, no!" He shook his head, stubbornly. "It is debt dey pay. Pompano, you tell. Me, I have seen *Lura Lou*. Sun he stand right over my head, hurricane all round me, water like glass where my boat ride. An' I see her plain—her hull an' sails like shadow on water close by me."

So Pompano told the story of Red Luck and his fair one, the lovely Lura Lou, and the debt they owe to fishermen.

CHAPTER TWENTY-THREE

Luck of the *Lura Lou*

THE schooner lay at anchor off the Florida coast in the dark hour before dawn. Red Luck was waiting for the signal to begin unloading his contraband cargo of one hundred slaves.

"Good profit for a short voyage," he thought complacently, as he leaned his elbows on the rail. "Let's see—three hundred dollars paid for them in Cuba; Le Comet should be able to sell them in the market for at least eight hundred dollars apiece. Slaves are scarce in Florida and the demand for cotton is unlimited; a fine healthy field hand might bring even a thousand dollars or more." He knocked his pipe out against the rail; the burning tobacco dropped with a faint hiss into the water.

Luck scanned the shore with a keen eye. It was 1830, and smuggling was a dangerous business; but it was profitable and exciting. He grinned as he thought of the two cruisers he had outwitted that day. They had followed the schooner for hours, hoping to trap him with the slaves before he could unload; unless they caught him with the Negroes on board, his boat could not be confiscated nor its owner punished—so read the law. But when the dark descended with a stiff breeze, he had lost his pursuers.

Suddenly, a light showed in back of the landing —once, twice, thrice—as though a black cloth had been dropped at intervals over a lantern; then the light burned steadily and Red Luck gave the word to unload the slaves. The longboats were lowered from their davits, and the Negroes herded into them. Red Luck climbed down into the number one boat, took the steering sweep, and ordered his crew of four to run out their oars. Soon the heavy bulk of the landing loomed out of the darkness.

When the boats plying back and forth had unloaded all the Negroes, Luck took the lantern to light the way, as he led the slaves, guarded by his armed men, to Le Comet's plantation. Le Comet, the aristocratic planter, owner of broad acres on the edge of the jungle, was his middleman for the disposal of black cargoes.

The quarters appeared deserted, but men emerged from the shadows and took charge of the new blacks. Luck demanded to know where the master was. On his previous visits Le Comet had met him in the grounds, welcomed him in his courtly French fashion, and led him into his house to feast on the best his great plantation afforded. Was the old man dead? No, Le Comet was not dead; but he had been forced to go on a journey in connection with his slave business. He suspected treachery somewhere; there had been threats because he made the planters pay so high for this live contraband. It was not a matter that a man could write letters about, so Le Comet had gone himself. As to Le Comet's absence, the explanation served well enough; but it did not allay Red Luck's anger at the personal affront to him. When the overseer added that Le Comet had given him orders to feed the crew, as usual, and added that their captain was welcome to seat himself with them in the white servants' dining room, Red Luck's anger became fury.

"I will go to the house," he shouted. "They shall cook the best food in the larder for me, or take the cost of refusing!"

There was nothing for the overseer to do now but speak peaceably to this angry man, who had armed rascals with him ready to obey whatever orders he gave them. Le Comet had made a mistake, but after all that was not any of his business. Antagonize Red Luck further, in his fury, and he might loot the great house of all its treasures and even burn the roof down, to say nothing of slitting an overseer's throat. A tough fellow, certainly, whose appearance corroborated all that the overseer had heard about him. Look at the man's bulk—six feet three at least, if he was an inch, with stormy blue eyes and red hair standing up crisply from his head, the shoulders of a bull, and long agile hands, well shaped to be sure, but able, nonetheless, to close quickly about a throat. Doubtless, Le Comet was right when he said that Red Luck had the mark of caste on his bold face and might have been sired by a gentleman, but that he himself would as soon cross him openly as fondle a cottonmouth. "Such men," he said, "are more dangerous than fellows of low caste, because it is also in their blood to take whatever they want as their lordly right, and to put down every challenge to their pride."

The overseer thought he knew why his master had not ordered a meal prepared in the big house for the smuggler, during his absence. There was his daughter. At this hour she should be asleep, not slipping down the stairs, trying to peek at a lusty-voiced stranger calling for fowls and wine; but who could say what a girl might do? Well, it was none of his affair: one hundred new blacks were enough for his occupation. So he held his tongue and watched Red Luck stride off toward the mansion: an arrogant and furious man, whose desires were his only law.

Whether Le Comet's guess as to the smuggler's lineage touched the fact or not, Red Luck came banging on his door now like a king who acknowledged no subject's right to locks and bars.

He cursed the old Negro who had taken so long in getting himself dressed to open the door, brushed him aside, and entered. He was storming about Le Comet's failure to entertain him, when he saw the old man look toward the stairs and almost drop the candle. Luck turned swiftly in the same direction.

A tall woman stood there, one slim hand on the polished rail. She was young, though past mere girlhood, ripe and stately, with black hair piled high and held by a jeweled comb. Her dark eyes surveyed him calmly, with a mild wonder; and he fell silent. Now, Red Luck had known many comely women, both dark and fair. He could boast that they followed him like gulls after a ship: he never need raise a finger.

At this point in the story Cella interrupted to say that if so many women followed him, likely it was not for love of him but because he was strong and successful and able to feed them well. Love would make a woman act differently, she thought; perhaps it was in her mind that she had followed, not for glamour but for love, an outlander, on whom no other woman had looked so far as she knew, and one who was softer and gentler than any in her native swamp. Cella thought much that she could not shape into words. The young Cuban fisherwoman shrugged her chunky shoulders and asked what else such women could do, since they weren't able to swing a net for themselves.

"Let Pompano go on," said his father.

Red Luck could only stare at this beautiful girl who regarded him indifferently, indeed, almost as if she saw nothing, so little did her eyes make of him. It was plain that she had never even heard his name, for she repeated "Red Luck" after him in a questioning tone; a man to have no more of a name than that, and yet he in her home?

"My father would not wish me to fail in hospitality," she said, and ordered food and wine to be

set on the table, and all the candles lighted. He ate
hungrily, because he had kept his appetite for Le
Comet's spread. But as they sat there, without speaking, their eyes met, and at last he saw that a deep
light had come into hers.

"What is your name?" he asked, abruptly.

"Lura Lou," she answered. "Who are you?"

Red Luck told her that he was a smuggler, but
he held back her father's part in the business. A
Cuban, he called himself, son of a pirate and a red-
headed dancer from Castile. He was a man who had
fought his way up barehanded, with the sea for his
helpmeet. Men knew his name, back there in the
islands; his Cubans loved him and toasted him in the
wineshops.

"You are not a girl, you are a woman. But you
are not a wife yet, as you should be. Have you never
loved a man?" She shook her head slowly, but her
eyes did not falter from his; her hand fluttered up
and pressed the fold of white lace over her breast.

"You will love me," he said.

"That would be to break my heart. You are not
of my world."

"Nor are you of mine. But I will make a new
world for you. And I will bring such glory about
the names of Red Luck and Lura Lou that they will
always be remembered." He kissed her, and went
back to his ship.

"He was right," Captain Portygee interpolated.
"We remember him long time now."

When Red Luck came back with another cargo
of slaves, he asked Le Comet boldly for his daugh-

ter's hand. The old Frenchman flew into a rage. He was insulted, he ordered Red Luck out of his house. But presently he learned that his lovely daughter loved the man and was ready to marry him. Then Le Comet smothered his rage, and appeared to be willing to consider the matter.

"Do not push me too fast," he pleaded. "Lura Lou is the only child I have. When you come again I will be prepared to talk with you."

The business that had taken him away had not turned out so well. The authorities were really suspicious of him. Now this smuggler would have his daughter! Red Luck was not a man to cross openly; but Le Comet saw a way to get rid of him and, at the same time, divert all suspicion of slave running from himself. So he betrayed Red Luck to the law. And two cruisers rode the Gulf tide waiting for Red Luck and his schooner, which he had renamed the *Lura Lou.*

Le Comet invited the officers to dinner and led them on to brag of the great catch they would make the next night. His eyes glittered as he watched Lura Lou's face go cold and white where she sat silent at the table. This was a fitting punishment for a daughter who had outraged a father's pride—and added too much danger to a profitable commerce. He watched her go, with drooping head, out of the room and toward the stairs, as he and his guests settled to their wine and cigars.

But Lura Lou waited in her room only long enough to tear off her dainty gown and slippers and put on the clothes she wore when she walked in the fields. Then she fled down the back stairs and along the jungle path to the little fishing village near by. These fishers were Cubans and they were all Red Luck's friends. He would hail them as he came to the dock, "Amigos! Amigos!" and toss out sacks of Brazil coffee, Holland cheeses, spices from the Antilles, kegs of rum. "Eat and be merry. We are all Cubans. Blood is thicker than water even here, four hundred miles from Havana!"

She ran to old Manuelo's shack; he was a leader in the village. "Manuelo! Manuelo!" she called, and beat on the door, till he woke from his nap and came out. "We must hurry. Come!" she cried, "see—the sun is down—soon it will be dark. The schooner will be off the coast at moonrise, two hours hence, and my father and the officers are waiting at the landing. Luck will come in at the signal, never dreaming that Father would dare betray him. What shall we do?"

In answer the old man picked up the great conch shell lying on the table, stepped to the door, and blew loudly upon it. The weird, whistling wail sang through the little huddle of houses and the fisherfolk responded, pouring out at their doors, some eating as they ran, others pulling on their faded jackets.

The Cubans listened, their dark faces malignant in their anger. Lura Lou kept close to Manuelo as they hastened to the dock. The fleet sailed through the yellow sunset on into the dusk and the dark, showing no lights. The boats spread out fanwise so as to run no chance of missing the schooner. Pres-

ently a light flashed far out—the signal that the
schooner had been sighted—and Lura Lou bowed
her head in her hands and wept. All the boats showed
their lights now, and the schooner swung down toward them. Manuelo put the conch shell to his
mouth again and sounded the familiar note which
told Red Luck that he was among friends. The
schooner rounded to and lay wallowing in the swells.

No time was wasted in greetings. Luck's arm
was around the girl, steadying her on the heaving
deck, but his ears were for Manuelo; as soon as the
old man had dropped back into his own boat, the
schooner glided along. By a way the fisherman alone
knew, through island channels they could navigate
in the dark, the boats of the Cubans led the *Lura
Lou* at last into a small landlocked harbor. A few
days later some of the fishers, who were spying off
the mouth of the Suwannee, reported that the
cruisers had gone.

"Den Red Luck make his promise," Captain
Portygee said. "He say he never forget how fishermen save him. An' when he is dead, he say, his spirit
an' *Lura Lou* come to save Gulf fishermen."

The Plant Woman took a keener interest in the
tale because it was the only phantom ship story she
had ever heard in which the ghost was benign. She
knew many that told how the apparition came as the
herald of death or disaster. There was a brightness
on the folk mind here, a kind of sunny optimism,
which transformed the nature even of phantoms.

The sun set white in a blazing yellow sky the
evening Luck sailed, bound for Havana. He noted

it as a sign of bad weather but he thought little about it. He was too happy.

Here Cella broke in timidly, her blue eyes wide with an apprehension that had been growing upon her for some time. She must know what became of the slaves. Were there a hundred on this voyage? How did Red Luck feed them? With fish? It turned out that nobody knew! The slaves had simply dropped out of the story, after the wise fashion of legends, which can discard elements no longer needed to maintain the mood of a tale. Pompano said he thought they must have been landed; no doubt they went up the river and lived with the Seminoles, the way other colored folk did. She was content, then, and urged him to go on with the story.

Dawn saw the *Lura Lou* plunging into a head sea, which swept over her bows. All day Luck drove the laboring schooner, under shortened sail, into the teeth of the gale. The glass fell steadily. Night came and dragged on with the boat battering her way through mountainous combers.

"You know, it was late August—our hurricane time," said Captain Portygee. "Hurricane come from Caribbean Sea an' dey blow from sou'east an' den dey blow west—or nor'west 'cross Florida an' de Gulf."

In the morning it was worse. Rain came in sudden squalls. Luck looked up at the dull purple clouds, tinged with green and gray, which scudded across the sky. The next instant he was knocked flat on the deck with tons of water pouring over him as the *Lura Lou* wallowed down into the trough of the sea.

Her rail sank lower and lower. Luck clutched desperately at a cleat fastened to the deck and struggled for breath. He heard the cries of the sailors who were dragged overboard by the savage pull of the water rushing past. The schooner shook herself and rose. Luck staggered to his feet. He saw Lura Lou crawling to him across the pitching deck. He gathered her close and lashed her to him with a rope end and fastened them both, with two or three turns of the short line, to the companionway rail. The girl hung limp in his arms. She had used her last strength to reach him. Her hair was blowing like a black cloud across his chest. Her eyes were open and for a few moments more he looked into them—the eyes that had once made nothing of him—and saw that they were still calm and fearless, and, it seemed, content.

The wind shifted and Luck knew that the hurricane was almost upon them. It was dark as night now. A wall of water rose out of the blackness and bore down upon the crippled boat. The schooner was beaten down until the rails were even with the tossing seas, her hulk was flung high out of the water. Then the *Lura Lou* dropped back into the sea, lurched to regain her keel, and rolled over.

"That is the tale of Luck and the *Lura Lou*," Pompano said. "But there is no end, you see, ma'am, 'cause they're spirits now an' come back to help us. So drownin' wasn't the end for Luck an' Lura Lou."

An hour later the Plant Woman was alone on the beach with the dying fires. She lay flat on the warm sand and looked up at the purple sky; blazing balls of fire studded it thickly, and reflected in the dusky water. Not even the bright moonlight could dim their glory.

At dawn Pompano's father would take her down to Cedar Keys to catch the plane for the North. She had taken leave of all her new-found friends, though doubtless waving hands and voices would hail her from doorways in the morning. Cella had clung to her and wept a little, the starlight bright on her flaxen head. Pompano had led her across the beach, a gentle arm around her.

It was still and peaceful, the water like glass. The Plant Woman dozed off. A murmuring sound aroused her and she opened her eyes. A late migration of tiny feathered songsters was flying low above the palm trees. Their wings made a soft whispering above her head. Golden swamp warblers, she thought. They flew out over the water, making unerringly for the mouth of the Suwannee. The Plant Woman watched until the last one had disappeared from sight. They, too, were on their way home.

Bibliography

ONE of the fondest recollections of my childhood is that of my mother singing "Way Down Upon the Suwannee River"; so when the opportunity came to explore the headwaters of the Suwannee and follow its course to the Gulf, I welcomed the chance and enjoyed the greatest experience of my life.

Years previous to my exploring the strange green land of the Suwannee country, fascinating articles on Okefenokee by Samuel Scoville, Jr., had appeared in magazines. These I found of great value both as source material and because they presented a vivid picture of the low country. It was through these articles that I first became interested in the swamp, entirely apart from its being the source of the Suwannee River; among the popular writers for whose work I am grateful that of Mr. Scoville stands pre-eminent.

I have found only one book, up to the present, on Okefenokee: the *History of Okefinokee* by A. S. McQueen and Hamp Mizell. It contains valuable notes on the early settlers of the region and hunting stories told by Mr. Mizell to Mr. McQueen, as well as quotations from scientific writers about the swamp. It was from this book that I first learned of the swamp folk and about Dr. W. D. Funkhouser, who, it is said, lectured at the University of Kentucky at Louisville on his discovery of a group of people in the swamp who spoke Chaucerian English; Dr. Funkhouser was a member of the Cornell University party which explored Okefenokee in 1912. Investigation has proved that the swamp folk use many words which are found in the *Canterbury Tales* and in Shakespeare.

Through the courtesy of Dorothy Ebel Hansell, editor of the *Gardener's Chronicle*, I obtained from Dr. Ira Gabrielson, Chief of the Biological Survey, permission to visit the wild life sanctuary which now occupies a large part of the swamp. To Mrs. Hansell and Dr. Gabrielson my sincere thanks are due; also to John Hopkins, Superintendent of the Refuge, without whose help I could not have accomplished the work I set out to do.

After seeing and talking with the people of the Suwannee country, I pored over numerous scientific and semi-scientific books and journals, trying to assimilate every scrap that had been written about the region. I am anxious to acknowledge my debt to all the sources upon which I drew freely for information; the following proved of the most value to me in my work.

For a general description of the swamp "Okefinokee Swamp" by Dr. Roland M. Harper is by far the best I have found and offers the most plausible theory for the swamp's origin; this I have incorporated in the text of the book. The paper in *Popular Science Monthly* contains, further, an excellent bibliography of Okefenokee literature, which enabled me to consult the original sources. Of these Jane's *Handbook of Georgia* has a fairly full account of the Atlanta *Constitution* expedition for the exploration of Okefenokee in 1875; J. C. Bradley wrote about the Cornell expedition in *Cornell Countryman*, vol. 10; M. E. Carr and W. E. Tharp cover the swamp and soil in *Soil Survey of Waycross Area*, Bureau of Soils, U. S. Department of Agriculture, 1908; S. W. McCallie's *Drainage System in Georgia* cannot be ignored by anyone interested in the country, nor can Nesbitt's *Georgia, Her Resources and Possibilities*. Other articles of a more general interest are: "The Okefinokee Wilderness" by Francis Harper, a short article in the *National Geographic Magazine* which treats of the swamp, the swamp folk, and the flora and fauna in an interesting manner; "Deep in Okefinokee Swamp" by W. H. Thompson in

Forest and Stream, vol. 85; a story entitled "In the Okefinokee" by Louis Pendleton, published by the *Youth's Companion* for 1894, which is said to be authentic incidents of his brother's experience in the swamp combined with the fact that deserters are claimed to have lived in Okefenokee during the Civil War; and newspaper articles in the Atlanta *Constitution* and the Macon *Telegraph*. Many newspaper articles were written by Earle Greene, now connected with the Wildlife Refuge at Okefenokee. My search for material on the river region was almost barren of results, the only writing of help I found being Dr. Roland Harper's *Preliminary Report on the Peat Deposits of Florida*, 3rd Annual Report, State Geological Survey.

As a guide to the flora I followed insofar as possible the *Flora of the Southeastern United States* by the late Dr. John K. Small, to whom I am indebted also for a large number of reprints of his articles on the Florida flora. After a trip to the Deep South I spoke with Dr. Small regarding the various local names in use for the same plants and the different ways in which some of them were spelled, and he stated that this was typical of certain regions throughout the country. In the swamp, for example, hurrah bush I have spelled as I heard it pronounced, while in other localities along the river it is spelled hoorah; *clethra*, the common sweet pepperbush of the East, is called leatherleaf by the mountaineers and leatherleaf or latherleaf in the swamp, the latter because the leaves make a lather when scrubbed in water. I found useful the many plant articles by Dr. Roland Harper, *Florida Wild Flowers* by Mary Francis Baker, and the numerous references to plants and trees in various papers on other subjects, especially those of Francis Harper in his excellent article on the swamp mammals. The swamp folk, in speaking of Okefenokee, have divided it ecologically into certain habitat groups and call these islands, bays, prairies, etc.;

scientists, in writing of the swamp, follow the same grouping.

The best paper on the fishes is that of E. L. Palmer and A. H. Wright, "Biological Reconnaissance of Okefinokee Swamp," *Proceedings of the Iowa Academy of Science*, vol. 27. The breeding habits of alligators in Okefenokee are discussed by Professor Albert M. Reese in the *Smithsonian Miscellaneous Collections*, vol. 3; reptiles are fully covered in a paper by A. H. Wright, W. D. Funkhouser, and S. C. Bishop, published in the *Proceedings of the Academy of Natural Sciences* in 1915, pp. 107-192. In Paul Fountain's *Great Deserts and Forests of North America* he describes a trip into the swamp and devotes a large part of it to a description of the snakes and other reptiles. The swamp folk say that alligators grow to an enormous size in Okefenokee; and, in the Altamaha swamp region, it is claimed that they have been killed and found to measure nearly twenty feet; even in the depth of the swamp, where they are not disturbed by any human beings from year to year, I should think that sixteen feet—the greatest length I have allowed them—would be the largest. Many writers, such as Sass, Rutledge, and Sprunt have commented on the enormous size of animals and reptiles found in similar swamps.

I covered the country from the Altamaha to the St. Marys and down the Suwannee to the Gulf, paying especial attention to the bird life. As an authority I used *Florida Bird Life* by Arthur H. Howell, Senior Biologist, United States Bureau of Biological Survey, and followed his method of nomenclature. I was especially interested in the cranes and was disappointed to find no records of there ever having been white ones in the swamp, although it is a favorite haunt of the gray whoopers. Dr. Howell writes that, although there are a number of published statements regarding the occurrence of great white cranes in Florida, they are all indefinite. He says that Audubon confused the whooping crane with the sandhill (gray crane) and that Maynard, in 1881, said that some years previously he was assured that the white whooping crane occurred on the prairies to the eastward of the Kissimmee River and Lake Okeechobee. That they were once in Florida is certain, however, as Wetmore in 1931 states that the bones of the white cranes were found in pleistocene deposits at Melbourne, Seminole, and on the Itchtucknee River. Forbush, according to Dr. Howell, describes the mating dance of the sandhills in his book, p. 350, 1925. The "Birds of Okefinokee Swamp" by Albert H. Wright and Francis Harper in the *Auk* contains excellent descriptive material and a partial check list of the birds with many of their local names which are in common use. Maurice Thompson wrote also about the birds of Okefenokee, and his paper, "A Redheaded Family," is especially interesting. There is not so much material on the birds of the Suwannee River but Arthur T. Wayne's "Birds of the Suwannee River," *Auk,* is well written and informative. At the time I was checking on the birds Earle Greene was also making a list for the Biological Survey. Bartram's *Travels* contains many interesting notes on the bird life of the swamp region. William Vogt's *Thirst on the Land* is a plea for water conservation for the benefit of wild life and man. The books and papers of Dr. Frank M. Chapman, as listed by Dr. Howell in his bibliography of Florida ornithology, should be read by all interested in southern birds.

For general knowledge of the country I read *Beavers, Kings and Cabins* by Constance Lindsay Skinner, George Rainsford Fairbanks's *History of Florida,* the *Fountain of Youth* by Carita Doggett Corse, *So This Is Florida* by Stockbridge and Perry and the records of the Florida and the Georgia Historical Societies; also numerous newspaper clippings in the files of the New York Public Library. The *History of Ware County* by Laura Singleton Walker is a mine of information. Articles such as *Our Friend the Frog* by Doris M. Cochran in the *National*

Geographic, the work of Alexander Wetmore and many others writing in *National Geographic* and *Natural History* proved of untold value. *Florida Wild Life* by Charles T. Simpson is an excellent general book on the region.

Comparatively little has been published on the folk-lore or the folk songs of the people of Okefenokee. Some of it was probably adopted from Indian tales of the Seminoles and Cherokees, especially such stories as those about the bumblebee, the beaver and the phantom deer. Some of the folk songs undoubtedly were brought from England, others filtered in from the Carolina mountains or were brought in from the outland by turpentine workers and the like. All the folk tales and songs are given as related by the various folk. Their speech resembles that of other folk in America who still retain the flavor of old England in their language. The Seminole influence on the Negroes is apparent in the tale of the coontie, which is a plant of great economic value to the Indians.

The people are a fine, splendid folk living close to the earth. The incident related in this book of the Negro boy catching ducks is typical of the shrewdness of folk who live close to nature. I saw much the same type of thing among the Indians along the Beni River in South America; and the writer Richard Gill speaks of seeing a similar incident among the Caribs. I have not used the names of any real persons.

For technical assistance, advice, and information special thanks are due to the following persons: Mr. Roddenberry of the Reconstruction Project in Waycross; His Honor, Walter B. Fraser, Mayor of St. Augustine; Charles O. Maus; Dr. Raymond Ditmars; Dr. Robert Murphy; Dr. George Noble and staff—especially Dr. Bogart; Dr. E. J. Alexander; Dr. William Vogt; Mary Bray; the staff of Room 300, New York Public Library, especially Dorothy Miller; and all the folk of the Suwannee country.

Glossary

OLD ENGLISH AND SCOTCH WORDS

Bedrite: duty of the marriage bed.
Blakeberyed: astray; to wander at will.
Blowzy: a ruddy, fat-faced woman.
Couthy: from couthie, agreeable.
Flack: to flutter or to strike a blow.
Fleech: to flatter.
Flinder: a butterfly.
Gaston juice: gastric juice.
Gower: disbeliever.
Gramies: annoy or vex.
Hantle: a good many; a crowd.
Haskiness: harsh.
Mizzle: muddled or confused.
Moky: foggy.
Moldwarp: worthless, shiftless—i.e., as a "mole."
Mommick (mammock): scrap (used in sense of scrapping or to put out of business).
Mornglowm or mornglome: hour before dawn.
Palmity: much ado about nothing.
Piggen: wooden bucket.
Progue: to goad.
Puthery: sultry or close.
Rookus: to have one's ruck (anger) up.
Rud: to redden.
Servigerously: vigorously or excessively.
Scoggin: a butt for ridicule; also name for blue heron.
Snuddin': hurry.
Swarved: crowded together.
Throddy: well grown, plump.
Upscuddle: quarrel.

BIRDS

Bee Bird: *Tyrannus tyrannus.*

Bittern: *Botaurus lentiginosus.*

Blackbird, Red-winged: *Agelaius phoeniceus mearnsi.*

Buzzard: *Cathartes aura septentrionalis.*

Chuck-will's-widow (Whippoorwill): *Antrostomus carolinensis.*

Crane, Sand-hill (Whooping): *Grus canadensis pratensis.*

Cuckoo, Yellow-billed: *Coccyzus americanus americanus.*

Duck, Mallard (English): *Anasplatyrhynchos anasplatyrhynchos;* Pintail: *Dafila acuta tzitzihoa;* Teal: *Nettion carolinense;* Widgeon: *Mareca americana;* Wood (Squealer): *Aix sponsa.*

Egret, White: *Casmerodius albus egretta;* Snowy: *Egretta thula thula.*

Gallinule, Purple: *Ionornis martinica.*

Heron, Great Blue: *Ardea herodias herodias;* Little Blue: *Florida caerulea caerulea;* Louisiana: *Hydranassa tricolor ruficollis;* Yellow-crowned, Night: *Nyctanassa violacea violacea;* Ward's: *Ardea herodius wardi.*

Ibis, White: *Guara alba;* Wood: *Mycteria americana.*

Indian hen: *Butorides virescens virescens.*

Limpkin: *Aramus pictus pictus.*

Loon: *Gavia immer immer.*

Mockingbird: *Mimus polyglottos polyglottos.*

Mourning Dove: Turtledove: *Zenaidura macroura carolinensis;* Ground Dove: *Columbigallina passerina passerina.*

Osprey (Fish Hawk): *Pandion haliaëtus carolinensis.*

Owl, Barred: *Strix varia alleni;* Horned: *Bubo virginianus virginianus;* Screech: *Otus asio floridanus.*

Partridge (Quail): *Colinus virginianus virginianus.*

Quail: *Colinus virginianus virginianus.*

Rail, Sora: *Porzana carolina.*

Skimmer: *Rynchops nigra nigra.*

Snipe, Wilson's: *Capella delicata.*

Spoonbill, Roseate: *Ajaia ajaja.*

Swift: *Chaetura pelagica.*

Turkey, Florida: *Meleagris gallopavo osceola;* Water: *Anhinga anhinga;* Wild: *Meleagris gallopavo silvestris.*

Warbler, Bachman's: *Vermivora bachmani;* Golden Swamp: *Protonotaria citrea;* Prothonotary: *Protonotaria citrea.*

Whippoorwill: *Antrostomus vociferus vociferus.*
Woodcock: *Philohela minor.*
Woodpecker, Cham-chacks (Red-bellied): *Centurus carolinus;*
    Good-God (Pileated): *Ceophloeus pileatus pileatus;* Ivory-
    billed: *Campephilus principalis;* White Shirt or White Wing
    (Red-headed): *Melanerpes erythrocephalus.*
Wren, Carolina: *Thryothorus ludovicianus ludovicianus.*

FLORA

Arrowhead: *Sagittaria lancefolia.*
Azalea: *Azalea viscosa.*
Bamboo-vine: *Smilax laurifolia.*
Bay, Red: *Persea borbonia;* Sweet: *Magnolia glauca.*
Bladderwort: *Pinguicula elatior.*
Buckthorn: *Rhamnus caroliniana.*
Calla, Wild: *Peltandra sagittaefolia.*
Canna: *Canna flacida.*
Cedar, Red: *Juniperus virginiana.*
Chokeberry: *Aronia arbutifolia.*
Coontie: *Zamia integrifolia.*
Crow poison: *Tracyanthus angustifolius.*
Cypress, Bald: *Taxodium distichum;* Pond: *Taxodium ascendens.*
Dogwood: *Cornus florida.*
Earrings: *Limodorum graminifolium.*
Franklinia: *Gordonia alatamaha.*
Gallberry: *Ilex glabra.*
Golden Club: *Orontium aquaticum.*
Gum, Black: *Nyssa sylvatica;* Sweet: *Liquidambar styraciflua.*
Hurrah (Hoorah) Bush: *Pieris nitida (Xolisma lucida).*
Indigo: *Indigo tinctoria.*
Iris: *Iris versicolor.*
Ixia: *Ixia caerulea.*
Jessamine, Yellow: *Gelsemium sempervirens.*
Lobelia: *Lobelia glandulosa.*
Magnolia: *Magnolia grandiflora.*
Maiden Cane: *Panicum digitarioides.*
Maple, Red: *Acer rubrum.*
Marsh Violet or Butterwort: *Pinguicula varieties.*
Muscadine, Wild: *Muscadinia rotundifolia.*
Myrtle, Crape: *Lagerstroemia indica.*

Never-wet: *Orontium aquaticum.*

Oak, Live: *Quercus virginiana;* Water: *Quercus nigra.*

Orchid, Bee Swarm: *Cyrtopodium punctatum;* Butterfly: *Epidendrum conopseum; Oncidium luridum; Oncidium carthagenense;* Spider: *Habenaria varieties;* White-fringed: *Blephariglottis conspicua;* Yellow-fringed: *Blephariglottis ciliaris.*

Palm, Cabbage: *Sabal palmetto.*

Passionflower: *Passiflora incarnata.*

Persimmon: *Diospyros virginiana.*

Pickerelweed: *Pontederia cordata.*

Pine, Longleaf: *Pinus palustris;* Slash: *Pinus caribaea.*

Pitcher Plant: *Sarracenia minor; Sarracenia psittacina.*

Pokeweed: *Phytolacca rigida.*

Queen's Delight: *Stillingia aquatica.*

Rose, Cherokee: *Rosa cherokeensis.*

Rose pogonia: *Pogonia ophioglossoides.*

Saw Palmetto: *Serenoa serrulata.*

Scuppernong: *Muscadinia rotundifolia.*

Sea Stars: *Sabbatia grandiflora.*

Sparkleberry: *Batodendron arboreum.*

Spring Tresses: *Ibidium cernuum; Ibidium praecox; Ibidium gracile.*

Sweetleaf: *Symplocos tinctoria.*

Tupelo: *Nyssa aquatica.*

Violet: *Viola septemloba; Viola floridana.*

Wampee: *pontederia cordata.*

Water Lily: *Castalia odorata; Nymphaea macrophylla.*

Yaupon: *Ilex vomitoria.*

Yellowwood: *Cladrastis lutea.*

Index

RIVERS AND AMERICAN FOLK

By

CONSTANCE LINDSAY SKINNER

PUBLISHERS' NOTE

Miss Skinner's essay, "Rivers and American Folk," is included at the end of this volume for the benefit of those readers who are most interested in our American heritage, and who may want to know more of the idea responsible for the Rivers of America.

WHEN American folk have troubles which do not end swiftly, they begin presently to examine their own sources as a nation and their own story as a people. They forget about these in good times. But when they are hit they remember that a new story, like no other in the world, was carried in chapters and cantos across the American wilderness on a strong rhythm and they catch at phrases to console and encourage themselves.

From Maine to New Mexico and from Texas to Oregon, old phrases are being spoken and then newly turned. There is in a number of states a very keen interest in the earlier life of those sections and efforts are being made to interpret it, or at least to make some new record of it, in literature and art. A new record, that is, which shall bring the vital past into the living present, unite them; so that it can be said "this we were and are, and there is beauty in it."

The first necessity of our times, as they relate to letters, would seem to be the retelling of the American story as a Folk Saga; if only to make the parts luminous by shedding on them the light of the whole.

There are, of course, several ways of doing it. Forms came into being for such material long ago.

The two most familiar are the epic poem, such as the Iliad in which a great poet blended fragments of history and myth, and the prose chronicle like the Icelandic Sagas told by several bards who could speak in prose as well as verse. We are conscious of rhythm as we read the Icelandic Sagas, as if thought sounded as it flowed, and the land the Saga-tellers lived in seems to rise visibly and move about the characters in the stories. The American Indians were aware—at least, their poets and dancers were—that rhythm flowed out of their beautiful land to them, bringing them thoughts, helping them to interpret Nature, their past history and their present experience.

The natural rhythm moving the pioneer life of America forward was the rhythm of flowing water. It is as the story of American rivers that the folk sagas will be told.

There are several reasons for telling the great saga along the rivers. We began to be Americans on the rivers. By the rivers the explorers and fur traders entered America. The pioneers, who followed them, built their homes and raised their grain and stock generally at, or near, the mouths of rivers. As their numbers increased they spread up the valleys, keeping close to the streams, since water is an indispensable element of the sustenance of the soil and all animal life. The rivers were the only highways of communication and commerce between solitary hamlets. Settlement expanded from the rivers. To repeat, the first foreigners on these shores began their transition from Europeans to Americans as River Folk.

Naturally enough, the effort to make a whole interpretation of a few American folk in localities has played its part in opening up the greater adventure, namely a composite study of the American Folk as a nation. This interpretative study will be issued in twenty-four volumes by Messrs. Farrar & Rinehart under the general title of *Rivers of America*.

This is to be a literary and not an historical series. The authors of these books will be novelists and poets. On them, now in America, as in all lands and times, rests the real responsibility of interpretation. If the average American is less informed about his country than any other national, knows and cares less about its past and about its present in all sections but the one where he resides and does business, it is because the books prepared for his instruction were not written by artists. Few artists have displayed to him the colors and textures of the original stuff of American life; or made him a comrade of the folk who came from the crowded civilizations of the old world and entered the vast wilderness of the new by all its shining rivers; or thrust him, as one of them, into the clash of spirit with circumstance, under the green arches of beauty, from which emerged the democratic ideal and American individuality—"rugged" truly, in its loyal strength, sacrifice and self-dependence. He has not been led to feel himself a neighbor and brother in the foreign groups which developed into separate Little Americas; evolving their own lore by blending old memories with fancies kindled by the new experience and, as the groups enlarged and mingled and occupied wide sections of river-pathed territory, spreading their imaginative compound of pioneer and Indian folkways, stories, songs and myths like a rich loam over all the seeding-ground of this present nation.

The average American has been prevented from a profound self-knowledge, as a descendant and a citizen, and deprived as an individual of the thrill and inspiration of a dramatic experience, because the epic material of America has been formulated by the scholastics instead of by the artists. This is said with full realization that we can hardly give adequate thanks for the patient researches of the scholars, and may properly say a word in censure of those budding writers who went to colleges and drowsed through the history hours without hearing even a few phrases of the great rhythm pulsing under the berceuse.

What has caused the tardy awakening? Partly, of course, the depression, and the present war of soap boxes beneath the artist's window. But the deeper reason for it is found in the recent self-assertion of the American spirit as expressed in sectional fiction and verse. There is something new in the approach which indicates that the American writer's reliance on traditional forms and methods is coming to an end. The spade striking to the root today seems to be sharper (if also wielded with less concern for surrounding growths): the horizon is often no farther off than the farm fence, the foundry wall, the end of Main Street; and there is an intensive, meticulous, and on occasions tediously thorough, searching of the particular spot and of the minds of the few characters; for the aim, whether it hit true or not, is such spiritual interrelationship of folk and scene that the ground itself shall sound under their footsteps and the shadow of their bodies never pass from the meadow or the forge where they labor.

The historical part played by rivers in the folk

life is evident but it may be a new idea to many that geography itself determined that Americans should first live on and by the rivers.

Here the map of North America unrolls, and comes into the discussion; hinting that Nature foresaw the day when old world folk would feel the need of a new world, and the new world call for inhabitants, and therefore set about her topographical modeling of the major part of the continent, between the Rio Grande and the Arctic sea, with accessibility as her chief aim. She traced large rivers in deep long lines north and south, such as Mississippi and Mackenzie, and east and west, as Rio Grande and Missouri. Others she drew with a fanciful touch; like Ohio and Columbia, which mark the map in large, irregular loops with an angle or two. There seems to be little logic in their designs yet, on their careless rambles—Columbia is more erratic than careless—they make contact with scores of smaller streams and so gather huge territories about them. The modern map is too crowded to do justice to the free beauty of the watercourses. They should be studied from the early pen-and-ink maps of the fur traders, who set down little else; since beauty wherever found is significant, and nothing is more so, and these charts show all the land traversed, and its remotest bounds linked, with rhythm, power, and grace. Philip Turnor's map, the first ever drawn of the beaver-hunters' canoe trails in the Northwest, is before me. The slender curving lines of the rivers, with the lakes set in like jewels, make a design a master goldsmith might choose for an empress's necklace.

In the heyday of the beaver trade, rivers opened

most of the territory between the Arctic coast and the Mexican border to the daring, singing voyageurs of the fur fleets. There was the famous Canadian route, traveled yearly from Montreal by the St. Lawrence, Ottawa, Great Lakes, and Lake Winnipeg to the Saskatchewan, which is commonly said to empty into Lake Winnipeg, but which, in reality, flows through its northern end and continues under the name of Nelson to Hudson Bay. From New Orleans the voyageurs went by the Mississippi and the Missouri, the true Upper Mississippi, to Montana: or ascended the Mississippi to its Minnesota headwaters, crossed into Canada by Rainy River, turned west through Lake of the Woods and English and Red rivers into Lake Winnipeg, and out again by either the Nelson, or the Hayes, thus following the whole of the water chain which connects New Orleans, La., with York Factory on Hudson Bay.

Mackenzie opened two new trails whereby traders in canoes could go from Montreal to the Pacific coast, having entered British Columbia by Peace River and to the polar ocean by Slave River, Slave Lake, and the Mackenzie. If they had a mind to go to the mouth of the Mackenzie from the mouth of the Mississippi they could do so, by water and the portages which were a part of all canoe travel.

When the trade was carried west of the Rockies, the favorite route led through the mountains from the headwaters of the Saskatchewan to that bizarre but navigable north angle of the Columbia River thrust up into British Columbia. From this point the voyageurs might choose to follow the river to Astoria at its mouth; or to swing eastward again by the passes,

coming out in time on the Missouri at Three Forks
and going on from there to St. Louis or New Orleans.

These were the routes of the great journeys, but
the singing voyageurs found many other water trails,
branching off from Ohio and Mississippi—the Ar-
kansas, Illinois, Red, Canadian (named for them)—
and all the smaller rivers lacing the western lands.
They had no thought of settlement, their aims were
fur and freedom, as they flashed their paddles in every
navigable stream and loosed more than a thousand
new songs on the air to the rhythms of new waters.
Yet little as they thought it (and how much less
would they have desired it!) they were opening a
continent to the Folk. By the shining, running rivers,
which had inspired men to sing in the wilderness,
entered "a great number of weake and distressed soules,
scattered, poor and persecuted," to grow strong and
confident upon their banks. In which connection, let
us recall that long before voyageurs caroled of "good
wind and swift water," an Indian poet sang propheti-
cally:—

> Bright with flashing light the distant line
> Runs before us, swiftly runs,
> River runs, winding, flowing through the land . . .
> Water brings to us the gift of strength.

Good reasons are found then, in geography and
history, for telling the American Folk Saga beside the
rivers. In this literary series, however, and it should be
emphasized that the *Rivers of America* is literary, as
distinct from historical, other reasons are paramount.

The special function of literature is to diffuse
enchantment without which men's minds become

shrunken and cold. There is a magic in rivers, beyond their gleaming beauty. They are unending rhythm; even when winter closes over them, in the mind, like remembered verse, they are still flowing. They are the motion in the still land, the vital fluid coursing through the clay body. To the first American, the Red Man, seeing them ever flowing away, yet ever there, they were mystery and wonder and beckoning—"That broad water, that flowing water! My mind wanders across it." Rivers symbolized life to him, as they have to other primitive poets in other lands. Our rivers typify for us our living link with the pioneers, who received "the gift of strength" on the banks of American rivers; who there became American Folk "naturalized" not by artificial processes of law and politics but by fearless submission of their hearts, and by honest putting of their hands to work.

The American nation came to birth upon the rivers. Has the fact colored our temperament? Are we a restless people because motion flowed by us continuously in our youth? Are we optimistic, eager, imaginative, daring, and even recklessly experimental, because of the beckoning of the tides "bright with flashing light" which ran swiftly past our known shores into domains beyond our vision? Are we in any part what we are, because of rivers? Possibly only a poet would answer yes. Poets have written of rivers and men, blending the spiritual over-tones of both: Spoon River in our time, Kubla Khan and Sorab and Rustum of an earlier period. Poets had discerned the power of Nature to influence thought and character long before the geographers of our day—more power to them!— began to contend with the economists for the soul of man. The *Rivers of America* offers a new and stirring appeal to the imagination of authors and readers. It is like a light slanted down into the depths of the American consciousness, which have become obscured from us by confusion in the shallows.

It is, of course, impossible to tell the complete story of America in any one series of books. The *Rivers of America,* also, is selective, conceived within definite limits set by the basic idea, namely the rivers and the folk. People are supreme; events are secondary. This is natural and right, because past events in America have been peculiarly an expression of the Folk of America, in striking contrast to the determining events in European history, which have been more often set afoot by monarchs and ruling classes from motives that took small account of the masses. The folk groups have increased mightily since they first planted themselves by the rivers; they occupy large sections and these various sectional groups now need a new introduction to one another. These volumes will make the inhabitants of the Columbia River country, for instance, acquainted with those who live in the Connecticut valley, the people along the Gila with the people beside the Hudson, on the basis of their common origin as River Folk.

The idea of the *Rivers of America* is original, and the plan it dictates breaks with both the old systems used thus far in American literary and historical series; i.e., the chronological plan, which divides material into periods, and the topical plan which arranges it by subjects. The periods will appear in these volumes as the intimate setting in which the folk of the times lived out their lives. The topics will be there, too, treated as larger expressions of the folk's energy, initiative, and will to life and power; which is what they were, in reality.

Instead of volumes on shipping, cattle, the fur trade, etc., stressing their economic importance, fur traders, cowboys, farmers, lumberjacks, fishermen, shipbuilders, will be shown as pioneer folk being cast in new molds by their occupations; for these labors and trades were natural and primitive, indigenous to the folk life, the soil, and the times. The church, the school, and the assembly have their place in these volumes. Civil rights, God, and the primer were held in honor on the banks of American rivers. How many state buildings, besides the Capitol, how many universities, agricultural colleges, how many temples, today lift their domes and towers above running water? A large number. We can still find some of their modest forerunners—on the Connecticut River at East Haddam, for instance, where Nathan Hale's schoolhouse remains and the chaste spire of the old church rises, radiant under the sun and, in the dusk, cloud-white. Religion, arts, crafts, and folklore will be treated in these volumes as characteristic expressions of the folk mind. Religious sects will be handled in the manner of good neighbors who show courtesy to other folks' opinions whether they agree with them or not. The plan will be carried out by the Editor, who has selected the rivers and outlined the material, i.e., the special folk stories for the several books. Each volume will be fully illustrated. The series has two purposes, to kindle imagination and to reveal American Folk to one another. Its authors, illustrators, editor, and publishers are also "folks," absorbed in issuing the story they have discovered which has been, thus far, a lost version of a great saga.

Everyone, apparently, has his "revolution" today —the word makes nice large mouthing, anyway—and American writers and illustrators are entitled to theirs against the "economic interpreters" with their foolish notion that the belly is the hub of the universe and America's own bright and morning star. If, as we hear shouted from the soap boxes, the old America with its customs and ideals is on the way out, we can march to intercept it and seize its baggage for our own purposes. Before the citizen, who flees history books, and is justified, agrees to exchange the American system for some other he should at least know what he is parting with. He really has no idea: he has not met "the folks." To be sure, philosophies change and systems fall; and the present is wiser to forbid nothing to the future since the past, heady too in its time, sought to picket the present and is proved foolish. To the creative imagination, the poet—and all artists are poets whether they use words or paint—the impermanency of structures is relatively unimportant. The significant thing is the beauty they have recorded and the inspirations of that beauty which flowed by many brooks into the long river of human thought.